CRISIS INTERVENTION
ACTING
AGAINST
ADDICTION

CRISIS
INTERVENTION
ACTING
AGAINST
ADDICTION

ED STORTI
& JANET KELLER

CROWN PUBLISHERS, INC.
NEW YORK

Copyright © 1988 by Ed Storti and Janet Keller

Published by Crown Publishers, Inc., 225 Park Avenue South, New York, New York 10003 and represented in Canada by the Canadian MANDA Group

CROWN is a trademark of Crown Publishers, Inc.

Manufactured in the United States of America

Library of Congress Cataloging-in-Publication Data

Storti, Ed.
  Crisis intervention.

  Includes index.
  1. Substance abuse—Treatment—Social aspects.
2. Compulsive behavior—Treatment—Social aspects.
3. Interpersonal confrontation.   4. Substance abuse—
Patients—Family relationships.   5. Compulsive behavior—
Patients—Family relationships.   I. Keller, Janet.
II. Title.
RC564.S784   1988   616.86'06   87-30615
ISBN 0-517-56859-4

Design by Jake Victor Thomas

10   9   8   7   6   5   4   3   2   1

First Edition

Contents

Acknowledgments — ix

Prologue — 1

Intervention and Addiction — 9

Intervention in the Family — 27

Friends and Neighbors — 113

Intervention in the Workplace — 149

Appendixes — 181

    A: Interventionists — 183

    B: The Treatment Center — 194

    C: The Twelve Steps — 208

    D: Addresses of Treatment
      Centers — 210

Dedicated to my parents,
Eddie Sr. and Georgianna Storti

Acknowledgments

There are many I wish to thank but some I must. To *John Oliveri* for his help and friendship, especially on the waterfront. To *Rene Monroy* for allowing me to break out of my shell. To *Ted Little* for giving me my first internship as a counselor. To *Jim Fulton* for teaching me the ropes and allowing me to grow as a chemical dependency counselor. To *Father Leo Booth* for introducing to me the essence of true spirituality. To *Dr. William Rader* for being in my life when I was searching; to *Paula Jones* for placing me under her wing early in my career and sharing the podium. To a small group at South Bay Hospital in Redondo Beach, California, who on January 28, 1982, demanded that a book of this nature be written (*Melvin Wilson, Judyth Perks, Kim McKenna, Judith LaMont, John Strouse, Betty Stuard, Marilyn Sears, Marie Francia, and Judy Godfrey*). For my experience at San Pedro Peninsula Hospital, which I carry today as my clinical foundation. To *Stephanie Abbott Soll* for giving me the insight in going from one career transition to another. To *Olive Reed* for her support and unconditional love. To Memorial Medical Center in Long Beach, California, for allowing me to create and work within a wonderful environment. To chemical dependency centers throughout the United States for their comprehensive services; without them I wouldn't be able to offer the patient a wonderful voyage. A special thanks to *Gerry McDonald* for his friendship, love, and support and the unselfish hours he gave toward the editing of the clinical aspects of the manuscript. To *Geri Thoma* for her courage, belief, and trust in me and my work. To *Mark Gompertz* for his guidance, knowledge, and acceptance of this book. To

Janet Keller for her commitment to excellence and drawing the very best from me.

To my family, that I'm so very proud of, *Jo Ann, Karianne, and Kristopher,* for their love, support, trust, and always being there for me. Especially to *Jo Ann,* for never ever complaining about all the time spent away from home; because of her and our wonderful marriage I can give freely to others. And lastly to all the families over the years that have allowed me into their lives, trusted me, and let me truly grow as an Intervention Specialist. To the reader I give this book with love, and I hope you gain insight and enjoy its message.

Prologue

EPIDEMIC: an outbreak of disease which attacks many people at about the same time.

THOMAS PARRAN
World Book Encyclopedia

I'm frightened for the American public. It took about fifty years to get to ten million alcoholics in this country, but only **four years** *to get four million coke addicts.*

DR. RONALD J. DOUGHERTY
Chief, Chemical Abuse
Recovery Service
Benjamin Rush Center
Syracuse, New York

W e are in the middle of an epidemic of addiction. It is spreading

> geographically—*from urban into rural and insulated communities. It is spreading*
>
> economically — *among people of all income levels. And it is spreading*
>
> chronologically— *through every age group, from infants born addicted to heroin through their mothers' placentas, to elementary-school children ingesting "crack," to elderly people drinking their lives away in retirement homes.*

Today there are more drugs to which people can become addicted, more people trying them, and more people becoming ill with the disease of addiction than at any time in history.

Many explanations are offered for this rampant drug use:

- Availability. *Drugs, legal and illegal, can be bought any time, anywhere.*

- Attitudes. *We're living for the moment, and drugs enhance the moment.*

- Glamor. *Substance use has been romanticized in movies and on television, and many admired public figures are known to use drugs.*

- Role uncertainty. *The makeup of the population is changing; mechanisms of social control are changing; gender roles are changing. People struggling to find an identity seek and find oblivion in drugs.*

- Need. *In a technological era, many people believe drugs are necessary to enhance intimacy, quench anxiety, counter sleeplessness, increase energy.*

Although these factors fail to explain why some people become addicted while others don't, they do suggest why addiction is a growing problem. And as the addiction epidemic spreads, its victims are not limited to those who contract the disease. Experts studying addiction have confirmed that people raised in homes in which one or both parents are addicted face an assortment of severe psychological and/or physical problems themselves when they reach adulthood. Alcoholism specialists estimate that 28 million children have been or are being raised in homes in which one or both parents are alcoholics. No one knows how many children are being raised by the estimated five million cocaine addicts in this country, or the half million hard-core heroin users or the hundreds of thousands addicted to marijuana, amphetamines, barbiturates, and tranquilizers.

We do know only 15 percent of the people in the United States who have the disease of addiction are getting help. The rest will ultimately die of causes directly or indirectly related to their disease—and before they do, will inflict untold damage and pain on their families, friends, and coworkers.

I am one of the growing number of crisis interventionists

working to change that grim scenario. And I write this book to tell parents, husbands, wives, siblings, caring friends, and coworkers of addicted people:

- You do not have to stand by and watch addiction destroy the life of someone you love.

- You do not have to endure devastation of your own life or your children's lives.

- Through crisis intervention, you can act against addiction and motivate your loved one to accept help *now*.

Betty Ford is the most famous person who has talked openly about the effects of crisis intervention in her life. In the closing chapter of *The Times of My Life* and the opening chapter of *Betty: A Glad Awakening,* she re-created that fateful Saturday morning in April 1978 when her entire family appeared at her door accompanied by two people she had never seen.

Those two strangers, Dr. Joseph Pursch and Navy nurse Pat Benedict, had come to Mrs. Ford's home to lead a crisis intervention. Prior to that morning, they had worked intensively with Mrs. Ford's family members preparing them to create a positive crisis in this gallant woman's life that would motivate her to enter a treatment center. If Mrs. Ford's family members had not acted to create this positive crisis, it is my belief Betty Ford would still be drinking or using prescription drugs today.

Similarly, were it not for crisis intervention, I believe of the nearly two thousand people I have intervened with over the past decade, some would be dead, and the rest would still be drinking alcohol, snorting cocaine, shooting heroin, smoking marijuana, taking Valium, abusing food, hurrying toward death. And their families would still be living in twentieth-century America's equivalent of purgatory waiting for their addicted loved one to understand what is happening and at last act against his or her addiction.

It is not impossible for an addicted person to act against his or her own addiction. There *are* addicted people who experience such a degree of physical deterioration and/or emotional trauma that they are finally compelled to enter treatment centers or join anonymous self-help groups.

But many don't. And for them, the ultimate question isn't "Are they addicted?" Their families, friends, and associates know they are addicted. Many chemical-dependent people themselves acknowledge their addiction.

And the ultimate question isn't "Will treatment help?" It is a proven fact: treatment helps.

The ultimate question is twofold:

- How do we change the mental set of the addicted person so he or she will accept help?

- How do we fracture the power the disease of addiction has over the lives of family members, friends, and coworkers so that instead of enduring its consequences they will act against it?

Crisis intervention resolves these questions.

Chemical-dependent people accustomed to evading the endless negative crisis spawned by their addiction—ruptured relationships, lost jobs, revoked driver's licenses, financial stress, physical deterioration—are compelled, through intervention, to respond to positive crises and, by doing so, to face their disease.

And the very act of intervening releases family members and friends from the grip of addiction on their lives. By communicating their pain and outrage at this disease's toll, and by pointing out the only possible way to end its violation of their lives, they take the first step toward releasing themselves from it.

The number of interventionists able to guide people to act against addiction is increasing. Crisis intervention with addiction, like any form of crisis counseling, is a service performed for a fee. You will find a discussion of how and where to find an interventionist, what to ask about intervention, and how much intervention costs in the appendixes at the end of this book.

However, here at the beginning, I feel it is important to state that cost is rarely an obstacle to intervention. Once a family or friend or business associate or corporation is determined to act against addiction and initiates the process by consulting an interventionist, the interventionist provides expert guidance in selecting an appropriate treatment center, exploring funding options, and preparing family members to create the positive crisis that will liberate their own lives from the disease of addiction and save the life of their addicted loved one.

Intervention and
Addiction

What is food to one man
may be fierce poison to others.

LUCRETIUS
De Rerum Natura, I

Hannah leaned intently toward me as she told her story, her pale, plain face deeply lined by years of worry. She said, "Lon was driving one of the tractors in the field. He had a thermos of vodka on the seat next to him. Our four-year-old granddaughter, Missy, was standing on the tractor frame directly above the whirring blades.

"If Lon had been sober, he wouldn't have allowed her to stand there. I'd begged him again and again not to take Missy on the tractor when he was drinking. 'Why not?' he said. 'She likes to help her gramps.'

"As I stood watching, Lon suddenly swung his hat around and yelled, 'Hee Haw!' Missy jumped up and down, laughing. And in the next split second, I was running across the field after them, the way you'd run after a child about to dart into the path of a speeding car.

"Lon saw me coming and stopped the tractor. I grabbed Missy.

" 'Hannah, what's wrong?' he said. He had the most bewildered expression on his face. He truly didn't know what was wrong.

"Something seemed to splinter inside me. I took Missy back to the house and started making phone calls to doctors, hospitals, anybody I could think of who might help me. That's how I got your name."

Hannah's story has always typified for me the tyranny of addiction. I close my eyes and I can see those three:

Lon   — *addictively diseased.*

Hannah   — *passive and therefore enabling: the one who, by accommodating the disease for years, had given tacit consent to its existence.*

Missy   — *the innocent, potential victim.*

What is there about addiction that makes people relinquish their lives to it? I believe it's lack of understanding of what addiction is, which, in turn, breeds fear of what it might be.

Addiction isn't the first disease to arouse such dread. During the Middle Ages, the person with leprosy was considered not simply ill, but morally depraved. During the eighteenth and nineteenth centuries and on into the early part of this one, many people believed tuberculosis was a disease of the will caused by a pathology of energy. In our own "enlightened" era, there are people who theorize cancer is caused by repression of emotion, excessive reaction to defeat, failure, or grief.

Addiction is often equally misunderstood, and the effects of that misunderstanding are just as devastating. Addicted people will either deny they are addicted, as Lon did, or, admitting it, feel powerless to act because they see themselves, not the disease, as the cause of what's wrong. Those who live with the addicted become as confused, defensive, and desperate as Hannah.

That day in my office as she went on to tell me Lon had been a heavy drinker for more than twenty years, I asked what steps she or others had taken to help Lon face his alcoholism.

"I've tried everything," she said.

But instead of telling me what she had done to help Lon face his disease, she described many of the "enabling" activities spouses engage in which actually nurture it: camouflaging addiction by telling employers, neighbors, friends, even one's own children that the addicted person has some

12

malady (the flu, a migraine, a cold, an upset stomach) to explain why that person was absent from work or a social occasion; taking upon themselves the major responsibilities of running a household or a business or an office; becoming acutely responsive to the addicted person's mood swings; rescuing the addicted person in a very literal sense by driving when that person is incapable of driving, bailing that person out of jail, then minimizing, thinking, "Well, things could be worse."

Hannah went on, "Every time I threatened to leave Lon, he stopped drinking. As soon as I relented, he started again. He's been to half a dozen psychotherapists. He tried a self-help program and came home from the meeting one night and told me, 'Hannah, those people are boozehounds. The day I can't drink with class, I'll stop.' I guess he thinks he's been drinking 'with class' ever since. So you tell me, Mr. Storti, what do you do when you've tried everything and everything isn't enough?"

I talked to Hannah for the next couple of hours about the disease of addiction. I told her that even though a "quiet" epidemic of alcoholism has existed for well over a century in America, only in the last three decades—as excessive use of marijuana became rampant in the '60s, addiction to heroin rose dramatically in the '70s, and addiction to cocaine became terrifyingly widespread in the '80s—was intensive research undertaken to determine how and why people become addicted.

Many medical and behavioral scientists have concluded that addiction is a primary, progressive physiological and psychological disease. It is definable, describable, predictable, and, if untreated, terminal.

I believe addiction feeds off two major components. The first is the biochemical makeup of the addictive person (often genetically predetermined), which renders that individual acutely sensitive to mood-altering substances. The second involves the person's psychological traits, which are many; a

13

few typically include being excessive in many areas, needing immediate gratification, being obsessed by the need to do things perfectly, being unable to express inner feelings, having low self-esteem and an attraction to pain. Such traits make addictive people prone to seek life-relief in the very mood-altering substances their biochemistry intensely reacts to, as well as to defend their need for such relief. So when addictive individuals take a drink, shoot heroin, snort cocaine, or smoke marijuana, biochemical bonds are formed within them to the substance they are using. The effects of those bonds may be so subtle that it takes years before it becomes apparent the individual is truly addicted. Or the addiction can be obvious within a very short time.

Current investigation into addiction is also revealing that certain activities—compulsive gambling, excessive sex, playing the far edge of the stock market—can activate the same biochemical response chain in addictive individuals that drugs do. This is particularly true among individuals who have previously been substance-addicted, and it's believed the pleasure/pain receptor centers in the brain, once having been programmed, are especially vulnerable and will re-addict to the excitation—pounding heart, sweating hands, that feeling of being on the rim—that certain activities evoke.

Because it is often difficult to find treatment centers willing to work with behavioral addictions—just as, in the not too distant past, it was difficult to find treatment centers willing to work with addiction to food or cocaine or prescription drugs—the case histories dramatized in this book are focused on substance addiction. However, I am confident that as it becomes more firmly established that the dynamics of substance and behavioral addiction are the same, comprehensive treatment centers will be created with modules available to treat all forms of the disease of addiction.

Whatever form addiction takes, as the person progresses deeper and deeper into the disease, there are typical developments:

- Actual physical dependency results as body cells become so changed by constant exposure to a drug (or activity) that they malfunction when deprived of it.

- The alteration in feelings and perceptions which constant mood-altering brings about makes it possible for the addicted person to avoid dealing with unpleasant realities, including his or her own disease;

- The addicted person develops an unshakable conviction, called psychological dependency, that the effects of his or her drug activity of choice are necessary to maintain feelings of well-being.

From Hannah's description, Lon seemed to be experiencing all these. And though that made the outlook for him seem bleak, I told Hannah it was nevertheless not hopeless.

Addiction is unique among progressive primary diseases in that although *cure* is not achievable, *remission* is. Not "might be." *Is.* If you were to tell AIDS or leukemia patients that remission is achievable, you'd see instant ecstasy, because you'd be giving them back their life.

But saying those words to Hannah, I saw the disbelief in her eyes. And I understood. She had admitted and accepted the disease of addiction in her life, had given it the metaphorical equivalent of food, warmth, and shelter for years. She had, in fact, become as addicted to coping with Lon's disease as Lon was addicted to alcohol. It certainly wasn't easy for her to hear someone say, "But you didn't have to do that." The fact that she had done it was, for her, proof that she'd had to do it.

What finally motivates people like Hannah to revolt can be as superficially minor as a forgotten birthday tapping into years of stored-up pain, or as terrifying as Hannah's sight of her granddaughter in danger.

Hannah listened intently as I explained that remission is achievable because the destructive entity in addiction is separate from the person. A compulsive obsession to drink

15

or snort cocaine or shoot heroin doesn't cause physical damage and mental deterioration. It is the ingested substance itself that wreaks the damage. Remission lies in *not* drinking, *not* snorting, *not* shooting.

The founders of Alcoholics Anonymous understood that. In the 1930s, they began successfully combating alcoholism with their twelve-step self-help program structured around the tenet that recovery requires abstinence (see Appendix C). AA utilizes mutual support and individual responsibility to achieve that goal. Addicted people for whom AA works and works beautifully are those who are ready to acknowledge their sickness, accept the support of their peers in attaining abstinence, and search within themselves to find the strength to change.

Lon hadn't reached that point, and left to himself he might never reach it, might die first. But Hannah had reached her end point, and I was convinced that through crisis intervention we could make her end point serve as Lon's as well.

One other thing I wanted Hannah to understand was the consistent pattern of addiction that identifies it as irrefutably as an X ray identifies a broken bone. So many people go on living with addiction, telling themselves their husband or wife or child or parent isn't truly an addict. By doing that during the early years of her marriage, Hannah had slowly but inexorably shaped her life around Lon's drinking.

I explained to Hannah that if the pattern is there, the disease is there:

PATTERN FOR ADDICTION

OBSESSIVE/COMPULSIVE
USE OF
MOOD-ALTERING
SUBSTANCE OR ACTIVITY

(alcohol)   (sex)
(heroin)   (gambling)
(cocaine)   (work)
(marijuana)
(food)
(prescription drugs)

+

LIFE PROBLEM WITH USE OF SUBSTANCE OR ACTIVITY

+

DENIAL OF LIFE PROBLEM AND CONTINUED USE OF SUBSTANCE
OR ACTIVITY

=

ADDICTION

I know that pattern well. Like Lon, I was born with the disease of addiction. In childhood, my disease of addiction manifested in addiction to food. I ate my way through frustration so often that I became overweight. Other children called me Tubby, Lardo, Fatso. But the comfort I derived from food was more powerful than the shame—a warning of things to come.

As a young adult, I transferred my relief-seeking drive to alcohol, and I know beyond any doubt that *my* response to drinking alcohol is different from a nonaddictive person's. I possess the psychological traits so many addictive people do, and I recognize them instantly in others, not simply because I have them but because I encounter them over and over and over again in the addicted people I intervene with. I know from personal experience that turned inward, these traits nurture addiction and negativity, but turned outward, they can instill a life with meaning and purpose. That's what happened to me.

17

In my late twenties, while working as a longshoreman on the waterfront, I was compelled to face my alcoholism by a life-threatening series of events. Through this acute life crisis, I became the one out of ten alcoholics energized to act, on his own volition, against his disease. I joined an anonymous self-help group, struggled to put my alcoholism in remission by attaining abstinence, and then entered therapy and began working to come to terms with and rechannel my addictive personality traits.

Subsequently, I experienced what so many addicted people in recovery do: I was able to use the obsessive drive and energy that had once fed my alcoholism to sustain positive forces in my life. I entered college and completed work for a degree in sociology. After graduation, determined to find out more about addiction, I became a probationary counselor in an institution for troubled, delinquent teenagers—many of whom were there because of their dependence on alcohol or other chemical substances. Working with these young people taught me a great deal about the effects of addiction on its victims but little about how to help them act against it.

Seeking more answers, I became a chemical-dependency counselor at one of the hospital treatment centers springing up across America in the mid-'70s as the epidemic of hard drug use spread. These pioneering treatment centers were focused on finding ways to activate and then accelerate and reinforce the recovery process. Because of my experience in probation, I was named counselor in charge of my hospital's adolescent treatment program. I watched teenagers who would have been labeled "incorrigible" in the prison I had worked in start taking steps toward recovery as a result of the dynamics of the treatment program.

Yet I knew few of these young people had entered the program voluntarily. Most had been cajoled, maneuvered, intimidated, sometimes literally forced into treatment by their parents. And when I started working with addicted adults, I found the same thing to be true. Few adults would enter treatment unless a great deal of outside pressure was brought to bear. And for every chemical-dependent adult successfully working on recovery, there were thousands who could not or would not act against their addiction.

Talking to their families, friends, and coworkers, I began to comprehend the devastating effects of addiction on people who were not themselves addicted. They would relate wrenching stories about broken marriages, impoverished life circumstances, diminishing quality of life, terror at realizing they were losing the person they loved. Then they would ask in desperation what they could do when their addicted relative or spouse or associate refused to visit a treatment center or even talk to a counselor on the telephone.

Searching for answers, I turned to an intervention model Dr. Vernon Johnson created in the 1960s while working with alcoholics. Using Dr. Johnson's model, counselors would gather family members in a series of classlike meetings and educate them about alcoholism. When that education process was completed, counselors would prepare family members to tell the alcoholic, face to face, how excessive drinking was ruining not just his or her life, but also the lives of others.

Although I knew these clinical interventions in institutionalized settings were highly effective with alcoholics, alcoholism, except in the late stages, can be a slow-acting disease. Weeks, if necessary, could be devoted to educating and preparing family members to intervene, and still more time to persuading the alcoholic to come to the hospital or treatment center.

The addiction to cocaine, heroin, and multiple substances that characterized the '70s and '80s called for swifter, sometimes immediate action. Acknowledging the validity of Dr. Johnson's basic intervention structure, I believed part of the education process could wait until the patient and family were in treatment—but that very quick action had to be taken to prepare and motivate family members and friends to intervene, and also to reach addicted individuals who refused to go near clinical settings. The solution seemed obvious: to prepare the addict's intimates as quickly as possible, then go wherever the addicted person was and assume a directive role in helping them motivate that person to take immediate action against the disease.

Traditional counselors told me that attempting to intervene away from clinical settings wouldn't be practical or even safe, because addiction to hard substances can create defensiveness and paranoia. What would happen, they asked, if a stranger appeared without warning in an addicted person's home to confront the disease of addiction?

I soon knew the answer.

The first few times I went into people's living rooms to intervene, I felt like an uninvited, unwelcome guest. Often I weathered explosions of outrage and betrayal, especially during my early learning years, when I made errors in judgment and accepted cases I would not accept today. But I learned from each of my mistakes, and as time passed I sharpened the skills I had and acquired new ones as I mastered the five steps of the crisis intervention process.

STEP ONE: THE INQUIRY

This begins when people call me, as Hannah did, and ask for help, either because a loved one is in a chemical-dependency crisis or because they themselves, like Hannah, have reached an end point.

The person calling is usually in pain, as Hannah certainly was, and sometimes too distraught to be lucid. Yet it's imperative to be immediately responsive to that person's need, whether it's for emotional sustenance, information about crisis intervention, or both. Otherwise, the caller already close to the edge may simply give up before communication can be established. I calm and reassure my callers, telling them no matter how severe an addiction crisis seems or is, a solution can and will be found; and I ask for a face-to-face meeting so we can focus on finding that solution, or if geography precludes that, I establish a time for a conference call.

STEP TWO: PRE-PREPARATION MEETING

This face-to-face meeting with the "core" participants—those who are intimately involved with the addicted person and want to act—is scheduled as quickly as the crisis demands, the same day if necessary. There may be only one person who is ready to act—a spouse, or a parent. There may be several.

I had my first meeting with Hannah two hours after she called me. I expressed my conviction, as I do to all my clients, that a solution to her crisis would be found and it need not be one that would further devastate her life. Many people come to me convinced they must divorce a spouse, dissolve a relationship, fire an employee, alienate a child. I tell them these major life decisions should be reflected on *after* the addicted person is in treatment—that time spent in treatment is a great clarifier both for the patient and for family members and associates.

During our pre-preparation meeting, I could tell that Hannah, though upset and frightened, was emotionally capable of undertaking an intervention. However, sometimes I decide the core participants themselves are in need of counseling or therapy to gain strength before initiating an intervention, and if that is the case, I will make appropriate referrals to therapists, or support groups such as ALANON (a self-help group for family members living with an addictive person) or ACA (Adult Children of Alcoholics).

If I determine it's appropriate to go forward, I make certain the core participants understand the risks involved. It's vitally important for intimates to know that when an addicted person enters treatment and begins to recover, their own behavior patterns will have to change to accommodate the recovery, and they will be expected to explore and extinguish their own "enabling" roles which may have actually helped the person remain addicted.

Intervention participants must also be able to accept whatever outcome an intervention has. While over 90 percent of the people I intervene with go into treatment, it's important for participants to understand that even if that doesn't happen, the intervention will still be a success. Once they have offered their loved one the best possible solution, regardless of whether that solution is accepted or rejected they will have taken the first step toward liberating themselves from the power of the addicted person's disease, and they are to get their own help.

I ask during the pre-preparation meeting what substance the addicted person is using, how long he or she has been using it excessively, and how debilitated the addicted person is.

If there is an employee assistance program and/or insurance plan available to the addicted person, I help the core participants find ways to utilize them.

Finally, I ask who among nonintimate but caring and/or influential family members, friends, coworkers, or employers might be willing to participate positively in an intervention.

In Lon's case, Hannah said she was certain their two adult sons, Lon's sister, and Lon's best friend would be willing, and we agreed on a time and place for a group preparation meeting.

STEP THREE: GROUP PREPARATION

I take a very active role during the group preparation meeting. I create a chemistry to bond the participants emotionally, get them past possible intrafamily deceit, help them acknowledge and deal with any feelings of disloyalty or guilt they may be experiencing, turn their anxiety into energy, and keep them unified on the goal of getting the addicted person into treatment immediately.

I tell families, friends, employers, coworkers, that the majority of people I intervene with are quickly and easily motivated, often even relieved at the prospect of entering treatment.

I also stress how important it is for the participants to be truthful during the intervention—to reveal their pain and express their love when asked.

As sharply as I can, I try to read the participants to determine those I will be able to connect with at crucial moments.

In Lon's group, I could tell his two sons and his sister were so thankful steps were being taken to cope with Lon's drinking that I would be able to connect with them easily.

The best friend was more resistant. He felt his participation in an intervention would be a breach of his close friendship with Lon. However, when I explained the grim future that would be the only possible outcome of doing nothing about Lon's drinking, he began to see his participation as an act of caring rather than betrayal.

As I do in all my group preparation meetings, I discussed admission arrangements at the treatment center and how we would get Lon there.

I acknowledged Lon could become outraged, refuse to go into treatment, even run away from the intervention. If any of those things happened, the participants could feel a sense of failure or self-recrimination, but such feelings would be resolved. The only true failure would lie in not intervening.

I explained that I would be the person in charge, orchestrating the intervention and doing everything possible to make it a comfortable and rewarding experience—but that once we began, there would be no turning back.

STEP FOUR: INTERVENTION

Because of all the preparatory work done in the group meeting, most interventions are anticlimactic. The intervention itself usually gathers momentum swiftly and moves to a close.

However, the first three to five minutes are often anxiety-producing for participants. At the beginning of Lon's intervention, his sons, his sister, his friend, and Hannah were all uneasy when Lon entered his living room and his surprise turned to anger after he found out what we were there for.

That's why, within the first moments of any intervention, I assert a dominant role as intervenor. This has the double effect of establishing that I am the person in charge and of diminishing participants' anxiety.

I'm a devout believer that most addictive people want help and simply need someone they are not emotionally involved with to tell them how to get it, and I am able to communicate that belief firmly and persuasively in my opening statements. I fortify my statements with concern and respect for the addicted person; then, as quickly as I can, I begin interweaving purposeful expressions of love and caring from participants. I paraphrase these statements when necessary to keep the focus on the goal of motivating the addicted person to enter treatment immediately. Most interventions are resolved at this level.

However, if the addicted person is unable to acknowledge the problem or is resistant to entering treatment, I concentrate on probing those issues.

If, after firm probing, the addicted person is still resistant or locked in denial, I use whatever leverage the participants have agreed upon—which may be a spouse leaving or a job terminated. Or, less drastic, a seed has been planted and we can acknowledge that we did our very best.

Hannah had stated firmly that she would leave Lon if he didn't accept the treatment solution. But that wasn't necessary. Before an hour had elapsed, Lon's anger subsided and he agreed to enter treatment.

In fact, the close of most interventions occurs within thirty to forty-five minutes. And even the difficult cases that last as long as two or three hours almost always end on a positive note. Once the close has been established, we follow the prepared plan for transporting the patient to the treatment center. In those few instances when the patient doesn't enter treatment, I remain with family and friends, helping them resolve their feelings.

STEP FIVE: FOLLOW-UP

After the intervention itself, the last step is follow-up. I go with the addicted person and family members to the treatment center. I ask one or two core participants to accompany the addicted person to his or her room while I stay with the spouse or parent or employer to assist in giving the patient's history to an intake counselor, filling out forms, and completing the admission process. I make certain the treatment center's staff has names and phone numbers of "crisis contacts," key people to call should the patient become extraordinarily upset or resistant during the first stage of treatment.

Before leaving the treatment center, I look in on the patient to satisfy myself all is well. I also have a short meeting with the core participants who accompanied the patient to the center to affirm in my own mind that everyone's emotions are stable, and to offer guidelines about the patient's possible volatile behavior during the first few days of treatment.

During succeeding days, I follow patients' progress by calling to check on their condition. And I stay in touch with family members to monitor their progress as well.

RESULTS

Over the past twelve years, I have intervened in airports, in offices, in corporate boardrooms, on private yachts, in a palace, and, of course, in people's living rooms. I have intervened with every kind of substance addiction—alcohol, marijuana, cocaine, heroin, prescription drugs—and with the eating disorders resulting in obesity, bulimia, anorexia nervosa, and in recent years with behavorial addictions such as gambling.

I have helped family members, friends, and employers motivate addicted people to take the first step toward recovery—getting help by entering a treatment center where they will learn how addiction has held their own and their intimates' lives hostage, receive guidance in putting their disease in remission, and discover ways to turn their obsessive energy toward positive life goals.

Through this intervention process, I have seen broken relationships mended, damaged careers reclaimed, and entire families healed.

Intervention in the Family

Home is the place where when you have to go there,
They have to take you in.

ROBERT FROST
"The Death of the Hired Man"

In past decades, the family was considered our most fundamental social tie. It formed the bulwark from which we faced the challenge and stress of life. It was the place where we looked for and found unconditional acceptance.

Some people believe the way we live now—our accelerated life pace, our technology, our mobility—has changed all that.

And yet through my work as an interventionist, I am convinced the family retains its healing and protective role; that much of the truth and goodness we currently find in life we find in intimate relationships nurtured with our kin; that the family is the one place we develop unshakable loyalties and an ethic of commitment and obligation. I so believe because these are the qualities I encounter when I prepare parents, husbands and wives, and brothers and sisters to intervene with an addicted loved one. During the hours they spend in my company before an actual intervention, family members reveal and share their fears and guilts, hopes and dreams, strengths and weaknesses.

They desperately want to help their addicted family member, but they fear telling that person how much pain he or she, through addiction, has caused. They fear having to acknowledge what their own roles may have been in perpetuating the disease. And they are torn by a sense of betrayal at "exposing" their intimate's addiction—to me, the interventionist; to the staff at the treatment center; to friends and coworkers and acquaintances after the addicted person enters treatment.

But they do it. They overcome their instinctive and natural resistance to baring their souls in public; they sustain and comfort one another as they would when facing any catastrophe threatening their solidarity.

They are a wonder to behold, and it is with a sense of gift-bringing that I share with you stories of family interventions I have done.

The O'Briens

Alcohol is the drug of greatest abuse in America. Compulsive, excessive use of alcohol has had, does have, will continue to have greater impact on the family than addiction to any other substance, and is often passed like a deadly legacy from generation to generation.

I have worked with hundreds of families damaged by this disease, but none affected me as deeply as the O'Briens.

Jed O'Brien was forty-eight when we met. Prior to intervening, I learned from Jed's wife, Adele, that Jed's father had died of causes directly related to alcoholism when Jed was seven years old. Jed's mother attempted to drown her grief over her husband's death in alcohol. Jed took his first drink in his early teens, and never stopped.

Adele's parents were just as addictive as Jed's. Adele's mother had been addicted to Dilaudid as far back as Adele could remember. Her father, a brilliant and charismatic trial lawyer, was a binge drinker who disappeared for months at a time during Adele's childhood.

Studies indicate that people with alcoholic parents who do not themselves become alcoholic have a 50 percent greater chance of marrying an alcoholic than does the rest of the population.

When Adele and Jed met, their addictive personalities cohered. Soon after their marriage, Jed told Adele that entertaining and heavy drinking were necessary to advance in his career, and Adele willingly complied, eventually becoming an excessive drinker herself. Jed and Adele had three daughters and a son during the first decade of their marriage. As the children grew up, their lives were gravely affected by their parents' alcoholism.

Adele first contacted me on a Sunday afternoon in early December. Returning home from church, I walked into my den and saw the message numeral illuminated on the telephone-answering machine connecting my home with my office. For my family's sake, I keep the ring on the "office" telephone turned off. But when I'm home I'll frequently check the machine and play back any messages so I can respond quickly to urgent calls.

I pressed the play switch on the answering machine and heard a woman's voice thinned with a veneer of panic. "Mr. Storti, my name is Adele O'Brien. I need to speak to you about doing an intervention on my husband. Please call me as quickly as you can." She gave the number, and there was a long beat of silence before I heard the click that meant she had replaced the receiver. I thought I knew what had been going through her mind during that beat of silence: "What can I possibly say to a machine that will convince this man to call me back right away?"

I picked up the receiver and dialed the number.

The same voice answered, but the "Yes?" was whispered.

"Mrs. O'Brien, this is Ed Storti."

She drew in her breath sharply, then said very quietly, "I can't talk now. Could we meet sometime tomorrow?"

I suggested 10:00 A.M. in my office.

She whispered, "Thank you," and hung up.

People living with addiction often respond in a furtive way when I return their calls. They've given such power to the disease, they lead haunted, secretive lives.

When I got to my office Monday morning, my assistant, Olive, was seated at her desk in the outer office. Olive is in recovery, too. A trim and lively woman now, it's difficult for me to envision her as "about the size of a walrus," which is how she describes herself when she was addicted to food.

She handed me a stack of phone messages. I shuffled through them, put the two most urgent on top, asked her to take all incoming calls after Adele O'Brien arrived, then went into the inner office where I work and meet with my clients. I have my desk at the far end, though I don't sit behind it when I'm talking to clients, because I don't like to impose that kind of barrier between us. Instead, there's a comfortable rattan couch and armchairs beneath a lazily spinning Moroccan fan light where we sit and talk.

My office, in the town of San Pedro, overlooks the Main Channel of Los Angeles Harbor, which serves passenger and freight ships from all over the world. While working on one of those freight ships as a longshoreman, I had the close encounter with death that made me face my alcoholism. Gazing out at the harbor through my office window, I can summon the memory of that encounter and the events leading up to it that began in my teens, when I first began to find relief from frustration in drinking. Gradually I became aware I drank more than my friends on occasion, and that my response to alcohol was more intense than theirs. But because alcohol softened the excessive demands I made on myself and the sense of failure I experienced when I couldn't meet them, I refused to worry about it.

In my early twenties, after working at a number of jobs that hadn't satisfied me, I decided to follow in my father's footsteps and become a longshoreman. I knew I would earn good money on the waterfront, enough to begin thinking about getting married and settling down.

My father, aware of my drinking, told me sternly, "Longshoring can be dangerous, so don't drink on the job."

I told him self-righteously that I only drank on weekends. At that point, it was true, and it enabled me to indulge myself

in every alcoholic's fantasy: I could drink forever by control-
ling *when* I drank.

But addiction is seductive. My Saturday/Sunday drinking
slowly expanded to include other days, too.

Although I never drank on the job, it was inevitable that
the drinking I did on evenings and weekends would begin to
affect my concentration and coordination.

Now, looking back, I wonder whether one of the things
that led me to become an interventionist is the fact that fate
intervened in my life at a time when things were getting out
of hand.

I was working with the night gang on a huge Japanese
freighter named the *Tokai Marui*—in a place I'd come to
dread, the ship's hold. It's a cavern deep in the belly of a ship
that reeks of past cargo, rats, bilge water, sweat. Usually I
could look up and see the stars. That night, a thick gray fog
was rolling in and I couldn't see anything. The winchman up
on deck began lowering a heavy load of steel pipe. When he
had lowered it about halfway, one of the sling cables sup-
porting the load slipped off. I didn't—or couldn't—move fast
enough. The edge of a falling pipe tore my scalp open. More
of the falling steel knocked me down, imprisoning and
crushing my left leg.

I lay in incredible pain, screaming in agony yet unaware I
was screaming until my foreman climbed down the ladder,
knelt beside me, and said, "Ed, we don't know yet how we're
going to get these pipes off you but you've got to stop
screaming." I did stop. Just like that. And as I lay there in
silence, I remember thinking, "Thank God I don't have
alcohol on my breath," something only an alcoholic would
think in those circumstances.

Over an hour passed before Japanese crewmen came
down the ladder with ropes and pulleys and devised a way to
wedge a block beneath the pipes and lift them off me. I was
raised out of the hold in a basket and put in an ambulance.

During the ride to the trauma center, I promised myself that if I lived, I would change my life.

That was more than a decade ago. Now as I wait for Adele, I look out my window and watch a tugboat guide a passenger ship through the channel to open water.

Adele arrived a little after 10:00. She was a pretty woman in her late forties—tall, but small-boned, with delicate features. Her prematurely white hair set off blue eyes thickly fringed with dark lashes.

I offered her coffee. As she nodded her acceptance, I gestured for her to sit down and inquired how she had heard of me. Seeming composed, she chose one of the armchairs and told me she'd gotten my name from the wife of a colleague of Jed's whom I'd intervened with a year earlier. She mentioned the name, but before I could put a face with the name, Adele's composure gave way and her eyes filled with tears. "I'm convinced my husband is dying, Mr. Storti. And I just—" Her voice broke.

I spent several moments reassuring her. Once she'd regained composure, she was able to answer my questions lucidly, even, I noticed, with a touch of melodrama.

I took out a pad and started to write.

"You'd probably better know," she said, "the abnormal thing in Jed's family and mine is *not* to drink." And she began telling me about it, starting with her own grandmother.

More than half of diagnosed alcoholics have alcoholism in the family. Of those, about 90 percent have one or more relatives who have an addictive disease. The biochemical makeup that renders an individual susceptible to addiction apparently can be transmitted through the genes.

In the disease of alcoholism, it's the quantity consumed by alcoholics that does physical and mental damage, as most develop a high tolerance. Many people can drink a glass or two of wine with dinner every night and have a cocktail at parties and suffer no long-lasting effects. But alcoholics consume so *much* alcohol to obtain the disinhibiting effect they're seeking that the toxicity inherent in that quantity wreaks havoc on the liver, pancreas, heart, and brain. It can also result in malnutrition, because while alcohol is high in calories, it has little nutritional content.

Adele told me she'd drunk excessively for years but had stopped abruptly when she went on a strict diet that didn't permit alcohol. She said, "When my daughter Moira announced her engagement, I took a long look at myself in the mirror. I weighed one hundred and eighty-five pounds—all bloat from the half-gallon of wine I was drinking every night. I didn't want to look like that for my daughter's wedding. My obsession with vanity suddenly became stronger than my obsession to drink, and I literally crashed into sobriety."

"All alone?" I asked. "No doctor or support group?"

She nodded. "Now I realize I should have had medical supervision. Because the first few weeks, I felt awful—didn't even realize I was detoxing. But I got through that, and I was thin and attractive for Moira's wedding."

I studied her intently. To stop any chemical-dependency habit without the support of counseling is exceedingly difficult. It can also be dangerous, and I thought she might still be emotionally unstable.

"After I'd been sober a few months," she went on, "I began to really focus on Jed's drinking. I became terrified at what I saw. I still am. When he gets up in the morning, he doesn't eat. If he did, he'd throw up. He has a cup of coffee, goes for a run on the beach, showers, has a double shot of vodka, goes to work, drinks his lunch, stops for drinks on his way home, and five minutes after he's in the house, he's passed out.

"I didn't see all that when I was drinking. Putting away my half-gallon of wine every night blurred reality. Finally I started confronting him with the fact that he was an alcoholic. But nothing I said, or did, did any good.

"Now I feel like I'm living with someone who isn't really there—only the outer form of who he used to be. Maybe that's why, inside my head, I keep planning his funeral."

35

I acknowledged to Adele that the chronic effects of alcoholism on long-time drinkers can evoke life-threatening problems: alcohol is toxic to bone marrow, alters cell membranes; there is always danger of alcoholic hepatitis, inflammation of the liver, pancreatitis, dysfunction of the immune system, heart disease.

And as I listened to her describe Jed, something kept nudging my memory. It seemed to me I'd heard the name Jed O'Brien before.

When she said, "He's in labor relations—a lot of the men he works with drink heavily, and Jed keeps up with the best," I suddenly remembered. Jed and I had met. Jed had been present at the pre-preparation meeting I'd held prior to intervening on his colleague.

Jed was tall and good-looking, with reddish-brown hair and green eyes. He'd ushered his associates into my office, and after they were all sitting down, told me he had to remain standing because of a bad back. So while the rest of us sat, he'd paced back and forth dominating the group—a role I could tell he was used to. He said he was sorry his friend Bob had been "benched" by alcohol, but drinking was a necessary risk in their profession, it helped them cope with the plotting and finagling they had to do. His eyes crackling, he said, "Just when you're at the crucial point and you think you've got the other guy, he'll slide out from under and come back at you with a new angle. I figure, what if we do have to have a few drinks to stay on our feet? The only thing they do is sharpen us up."

But occupational justification for drinking is a technique a lot of alcoholics use. I'd done it myself when I was working on the waterfront.

Jed hadn't been able to be present for the intervention on his colleague but I was certain he'd remember me and, when he saw me in his home, know what I had come for. Losing the element of surprise could work against my leading a successful intervention. I told Adele that.

Revealing the frantic will I would soon come to know better, Adele said, "I still want you to lead the intervention."

I asked her then how much Jed's colleague's wife had told her. Some people who have participated in an intervention will describe the process in detail. Others will say very little.

Evidently the wife had talked for hours, because Adele had an excellent understanding of the process.

I asked whether she'd thought about who she wanted to participate. She said she wanted Jed's boss, Axel Sears, to take part; and all four of her children would have to be there, because Jed would see any family member's absence as a lack of unity and might try to use that to defend his drinking.

She said the three oldest lived away from home. Moira, twenty-nine, was a junior partner in a law firm; Erin, twenty-eight, was a commercial artist; their only son, Charles, twenty-one, was a junior in college. The youngest daughter, Pixie, eighteen, a college freshman, still lived with her and Jed in their house near the beach.

I asked about the children's relationship with Jed.

She started with the oldest, telling me that Moira had just recently begun attending a self-help group for children of alcoholics. She said, "Growing up, Moira tried and came close to being the perfect daughter. She got straight A's, was elected to student offices, was a great help to me in taking care of the younger children. I think she believed being a wonderful daughter might make Jed stop drinking. Even after she got married, she still tried to be the best at everything—the most competent lawyer in her firm, the perfect wife. I think she still feels there is something she could do to save her father—only Jed has shut down communication. This frustrates Moira, but at the same time, she's relieved. Does that make sense?"

I said it did, then asked, "Who comes next?"

"Erin."

I could hear a note of exasperation in her voice as she said, "Erin's always been unconventional, and Jed liked that. As a child, she'd wear outlandish clothes. I never knew what was going to come out of her mouth. She hated school and sometimes she'd simply say, 'I'm not going.' Well, Jed allowed that. He'd say, 'Let her stay home if she wants to.' Of course, she adored him for it. She still does. Erin never wanted to mother him like Moira, or try to get close to him like Pixie. She simply accepts him."

Adele fell silent.

"And where does Pixie fit in?"

"She's the youngest."

Another silence.

Apparently she didn't want to talk about Pixie. I needed to know why. I said, "You mentioned that Pixie tried to get close to Jed?"

Adele sighed. "Yes. As a little girl, she would do anything to get his attention. Good things and bad. Be sweet and affectionate until he'd call her the best girl in the world. Then an hour later, she'd start screaming because he ignored something she'd said or done."

"And now?" I asked.

"Now, I don't know." The stubborn set of her mouth told me that was as much as I was going to learn about Pixie that morning.

"And Charles?" I asked.

"He's living up north, in and out of college. Right now, he doesn't have much to do with the family." Again, there was resistance in her tone.

"But you want him to be present at the intervention?"

She gave an emphatic nod. "We all have to be there."

I wasn't positive that was a good idea, but I suggested she contact her children and Jed's boss and set up a group meeting as quickly as possible. Her description of Jed made me believe he might be acutely ill. I told her we could have the preparation meeting Wednesday morning or evening at

Moira's or Erin's home or in my office, and she said she'd call me to confirm the time and place.

After she left, I sat thinking about my earlier meeting with Jed. I'd seen many signs of alcoholism in him that day. And scanning what I'd written as Adele talked, I suspected Jed now had to use alcohol in such large amounts it was interfering with his metabolic processes; in fact, he probably had to stay intoxicated from morning to night.

There was a soft knock on my door. I glanced up. "Come in."

Olive opened the door. From her expression and her hesitation—she didn't say anything right away—I could tell something was very wrong.

"What is it?"

"Miriam Jenkins called while you were in conference."

I was scheduled to intervene on Miriam's husband, Dan, the next Saturday in Arizona. "How bad is it?" I asked.

"He went into grand mal seizures last night," she said, "and died this morning. She'd like you to call her when you can." Olive went back to her office, shutting the door softly.

I sat for a while with my eyes closed. Miriam was Dan's second wife. She had postponed intervening while she tried to win the support of Dan's children.

I'd told her I didn't think that was wise.

But truly wanting her stepchildren's support, Miriam had told me, "I can persuade them. Just give me a month."

I could call up a memory of every condolence call I'd made to people who had waited too long. It's always difficult, because they're overwhelmed by guilt. I do my best to remove that burden. But each time I go through this, my sense of urgency is heightened. And the next time I'm presented with a severe-stage case of alcoholism, I try my hardest to persuade the family to act *now*.

I was on the phone with Miriam for almost an hour. When I hung up, Olive brought me the stack of messages that had accumulated during the morning—a mix of calls from people in crises who wanted me to call them back as soon as possible, and progress reports from treatment centers about people I'd intervened with. I was absorbed for much of the day on the telephone, and it was late afternoon when Olive buzzed me on the intercom. "Can you talk to Adele O'Brien? She says it's urgent."

I said yes and pressed the lighted call button.

The edge of panic was back in Adele's voice as she told me she was having trouble getting people together for the group preparation meeting. Jed's boss was involved in a crucial strike negotiation up north and wouldn't be able to get away until Saturday.

Also her son, Charles, in the middle of final exams at college, had told her he couldn't make it until Saturday either.

She asked whether I could meet face to face with just her and the daughters Wednesday, prepare the others by phone, and schedule Jed's intervention for Saturday.

Weighing my answer, I realized I was gouging black marks on my O'Brien note tablet—always a sign of resistance on my part. I knew that if I hadn't been convinced Jed was at a critical stage, and if Miriam Jenkins's case weren't so fresh in my mind, I'd be trying to slow things down.

I'd be proceeding cautiously partly because my meeting with Adele had made me aware of probable deep pathology existing in the O'Brien family. Jed was, and Adele had been, alcoholic for years. Children of alcoholics learn to use denial as a defense mechanism just as their parents do, to deaden emotion and avoid pain. Marking out self-protective roles to play in their families, they become like performers who never get to go off stage. But maintaining such roles is also what makes the chaos in their lives manageable. From what Adele had told me, I suspected Moira had played the "hero"—the one who tried to save everybody else by sacrificing herself. Erin sounded like the "rebel." Pixie and Charles were unknowns, but the subtle alteration in Adele's voice when she spoke about them made me suspect trouble.

Also, having to prepare two participants by phone bothered me. I'm never satisfied preparing people by phone. I prefer face-to-face contact so I can deal with positive and negative feelings and take advantage of the bond a group meeting generates.

But addiction crises can be equivalent to watching someone hurry toward a precipice. So I told Adele, "Yes."

A few minutes later, Olive stuck her head in the door, said she was going home. I glanced at the clock: 5:37. I sighed and put down my pencil. "Me too."

I gathered up my phone messages to take with me and go through later in the evening. Then Olive and I locked up and left together.

I watched my assistant walk toward her car. Three years ago, she'd gone on eating binges that left her bloated and ill. Now she seemed a sturdy figure in the gathering dusk. Her commitment to the hard work of recovery had changed her life.

The four O'Brien women arrived at my office at 10:00 sharp on Wednesday morning. I sensed at once I was heading into a storm. I could feel strong discord among them, as though they'd ridden in the same car squabbling all the way.

Moira was a small, pretty woman whose appealing manner invited me to like and approve of her. But beneath that, I glimpsed the deep tiredness of someone who'd tried to pick up the pieces of her family too many times.

The second daughter, Erin, strongly resembled Adele, only without the melodrama. It became apparent she'd learned to hide behind humor as she said, "Ed, I want you to know the resemblance between us three and the Brady Bunch girls is purely coincidental."

I observed her protective attitude toward her younger sister, Pixie, a startlingly beautiful young woman with silvery-blond hair. But the shadows beneath Pixie's eyes worried me, and so did her extreme nervousness.

When we were seated facing one another, I felt none of the daughters wanted to be here, and I guessed that just as Jed's alcoholism had reached a critical stage, so had the relationships within this family.

I said to the daughters, "Your mother has told me she believes your father is acutely ill. Do you all agree?"

Moira said, "Yes," and after a moment, Erin did, too.

Several moments passed before Pixie gave a grudging nod.

I pressed on. "And you're all willing to be present Saturday morning while I talk to your father and get him to agree to enter a treatment center?"

Adele answered, "The girls have given me their word—they'll be there."

I said as gently as I could, "I need to know whether they *want* to be there."

Again an immediate "Yes" from Moira.

With an irritable little shrug, Erin said, "Sure, but I think you mean while you *try* to get him to agree."

"He won't go," Pixie said. "No matter what."

I looked at her, and she averted her eyes.

I asked, "Why do you feel your father won't accept help, Pixie?"

"He can't. He's too stubborn and proud. He wants to solve all his own problems. I wait up for him almost every night, sit at the kitchen table and have a beer with him, try to talk to him, and he just—the next day he doesn't even remember." Her voice trailed off.

As the only child of two alcoholics, I was positive Jed had shut down his feelings and taught himself not to "need" anyone. And of course his own drinking insulated him even more. I said, "Pixie, alcohol has put your father out of your reach."

"Isn't that why we're here?" Moira said quietly.

"Well, it's a last stand as far as I'm concerned," Erin stated.

"Meaning?" I asked.

"This is it—the last scheme of my mother's I'm going along with. It's probably hopeless. Look, I have a husband and a career and I want to get on with my life."

"When have you ever done anything else?" Adele snapped.

"Thank you, Mother."

It was an exchange that tapped into old wounds, and Adele, her blue eyes snapping with anger, jolted all of us by saying, "If this intervention doesn't work and your father refuses treatment, I want you all to know I'm divorcing him."

Moira and Erin looked at each other.

Pixie's eyes were panic-stricken. "No, Mother!"

Erin quickly put her hand on her sister's, but Pixie didn't notice. "You can't walk out on him. He needs help now more than he ever has!"

Early in my career, I learned interventions can bog down when the interventionist tries to fix everyone during a preparation meeting. So now I move people past family feuding by keeping their attention focused on the person I'm intervening with. I said, "The important thing is to intervene as quickly as possible and get Jed into treatment. Once that's accomplished, you'll all be involved in intensive family counseling, and that will be an appropriate time to weigh major life decisions."

Adele and Erin and Moira grew calmer, but Pixie continued to seem so upset and miserable that I wished I could focus on her for the next few hours. But Jed was the key, and it was time to verbalize something that had been growing clearer in my mind since I'd seen how much turmoil there was in this family.

I believed Adele could be verging on a breakdown. Pixie, I also saw, was ill. Either could go off on a tangent during the intervention and cause Jed to explode. I wanted to offer them an escape hatch, for their own sakes as well as his.

I said, "Adele, during all this time you've been confronting Jed, you've probably said everything possible about his drinking. It isn't going to help to repeat any of it. Saturday morning, we want him to hear things he's never heard before. If you'd rather not be present, that's all right."

She just looked puzzled. "But I have to be there. We all do."

She was determined to uphold the unity of the clan, even if it didn't exist. I wasn't surprised. People in her predicament often cling to structures that are no longer viable. I said, "Then I think it would be best if you don't say much during the intervention."

And I turned to Pixie. "I don't want you to say anything either."

"Why not me?" Her eyes immediately filled with tears. "I'm not deserting him."

"Because you're in tremendous pain, and you might communicate something other than your love and concern to your father. Also, you might undo what you were trying to do."

"It's okay, Pixie." Erin again put her hand on her sister's. "Moira and I can do it. You'll see."

I felt on firm ground with both older daughters. Moira's calmness during this stormy meeting made me believe she had already begun coming to terms with her feelings toward Jed in the self-help ACA meetings she was attending.

And the deep affection Adele had told me Erin felt for her father became evident when she asked, "What will you do if he won't go in for treatment? I mean, I'd hate to see him humiliated."

"I always find a way to let people hold on to their pride," I said.

"Even if it fills a whole room?"

I nodded. "Especially then."

Moira and Erin and I went on to discuss things I felt it would be helpful for them to say to Jed. Pixie and Adele listened, and Pixie's eyes were so tormented, I believed she was fragmented and wondered if she really would be able to remain controlled during the intervention.

I stated and restated my strategy, stressing the final message we had to project—but I continued to feel a gnawing uneasiness, knowing because of the pathology in the family, I would have to dominate the intervention.

Near the end of the meeting, I again asked Adele to tell me about Charles, hoping he'd be an asset.

The spiritless way she responded confirmed how spent she was. She said her son's relationship with Jed had always been shaky and now there was practically no contact between them. But that was one of the reasons she wanted Charles present—she hoped the intervention would form new bonds.

I did, too; but I knew Jed and Adele had been several years into their alcoholism by the time Charles and Pixie were born, and I had seen the shape Pixie was in, so I was gravely concerned about Charles's stability. I hoped I could get a clearer picture when I called him.

The O'Brien women left my office a little after noon. I was relieved to see Olive hadn't gone out to lunch yet and asked her to stay and take incoming calls while I tried to reach Axel Sears and Charles.

As I was heading through the door back into my office, Olive said, "Ed . . ."

I turned. "Hm?"

"The youngest O'Brien—Pixie?"

"Yes?"

"Do you think she might be bulimic?"

Recovering addicts can usually spot someone who is addicted to the same substance they once were.

I said, "I don't know. Maybe." I'd begun to see Pixie as a young woman mired in childhood. She had grown up with two sisters who wore their protective "hero" and "rebel" roles like coats of armor, and the only thing she could figure out to do was strive for attention by remaining a child. I just hoped intervening on Jed would open doors for the whole family. They were in the worst tangle I'd seen in years.

I went on into my office and called Axel first, because Adele had told me the best time to reach him would be when the strike negotiators broke for lunch. He was in, and his secretary connected me at once.

"I'm damn glad Adele has decided to intervene," Axel told me. "If she hadn't, *I* might have. Jed's been slipping badly on the job."

I asked Axel if he would tell Jed that during the intervention if I judged it necessary, and he said, "Absolutely." By the time we finished our conversation, I felt confident he'd be a strong ally.

Charles was another matter.

He answered on the seventh ring, just when I was about to hang up, and sounded as if he were speaking from inside a tunnel. Instantly, I realized Charles was stoned.

I couldn't pin him down on a thing. His answers consisted of "Maybe" and "I suppose so." He committed himself only to being present for the intervention, because his mother had made him promise.

I felt he'd chosen the "lost person" role to play in his family—disappearing inside himself to avoid the chaos. Some "lost" children of alcoholics never do risk personal relationships, since their primary goal in life is to avoid further pain.

Dismayed after my conversation with Charles, I wondered whether I should try again to convince Adele that she, Pixie, and Charles weren't going to contribute anything positive to the intervention. Yet even as my hand reached for the phone, I knew I'd run into her obsession with "the clan." I gave it up.

The O'Brien home was a one-hour drive north of Palos Verdes. About a mile before the entrance to their beachside residential community, I came to a place where the road narrowed abruptly and had to slow almost to a stop in front of a yellow warning sign that read: "Landslide Area. Constant land movement next 5.5 miles. USE EXTREME CAUTION." Beyond the sign, the road turned into a blacktop roller coaster full of dips and rises where the surface had buckled from intense land activity beneath. I couldn't help thinking how apt it was for the O'Briens to live in such a place: physical beauty covering chaos.

I'd arranged to meet Axel Sears and the O'Brien children at the entrance gate; Adele had said she'd remain in the house with Jed to make sure he didn't go anywhere. Turning in at the gate, I saw Charles O'Brien for the first time—a tall, well-proportioned young man with dark curly hair—standing with his three sisters. But I didn't see Axel. I parked and got out of my car.

Moira smiled and came forward to greet me, saying, "Good morning." But when she shook my hand, hers was clammy, and behind the sunglasses she wore, I glimpsed her anxious eyes.

Erin looked at me silently, then over at Pixie, who sang out, "Helloooo, Mr. Storti . . . how're yooou?" She hummed a current rock tune and danced a few steps, trying unsuccessfully to get Charles to dance with her—hardly your typical pre-intervention behavior. Clearly, she was on something.

Charles remained subdued as Moira introduced us. I talked with him only briefly, because his pale complexion and trembling hands confirmed my speculation he was unwell. This made me sharply aware that there were only three people I would be able to call on during this intervention, and one of them was missing. I wondered if Axel had somehow misunderstood and gone directly to the house. We waited for about ten minutes, but he still didn't come.

I said with determined cheerfulness, "Come on, O'Briens, let's go. When we get to the house, don't walk in with your heads hanging. Smile. Look your father in the eye. Remember, you're bringing him a gift."

Moira told me the house was about two miles from the

entrance gate, and she would lead the way in her car. Pixie and Charles got in with her, and Erin rode with me.

As I turned on the ignition, she said, "Listen, Charles is hung over. Pixie is behaving like an inmate. Axel could be a no-show. Why don't we all go out for a Big Mac?"

I smiled. "Hey. It'll be fine. You'll see."

She gave that impatient little shrug I'd noticed during the preparation. "Fine, huh? God, you and Moira are a matched pair."

Ahead of us, I watched Pixie roll down the window of Moira's car and lean out. She waved to Erin and me, her silvery-blond hair blowing in the wind, and shouted something we couldn't hear.

Erin glanced at me and said quietly, "You know, if I were to choose who in our family should be intervened with, I'd say first Pixie, then Dad, then Charles. I mean, my dad's lived fifty years. The way things are going, Pixie isn't going to make it half that long."

I could tell she needed to talk about it. "I gather you two are close."

A wry smile. "I don't know why she picked me instead of Moira as her surrogate mother. I'm certainly not good at it. She started confiding in me when she entered junior high. I was shocked at some of the things she told me. I couldn't understand why she didn't have the same kind of ethics I'd had when I was her age. I'd misbehaved a little, but I was always cautious about doing anything harmful to myself or self-destructive. Pixie didn't seem to have those kinds of fears. She'd cut whole weeks of classes. She even got arrested once for mouthing off at a policeman when the boy she was with was pulled over for drunk driving. God, sometimes it's like I can see 'This person will self-destruct in one year' stamped across her forehead. Shall I say more? Or have you already figured it out?"

"Heavy into marijuana and alcohol. My assistant, Olive, thought she might be bulimic."

After a silence, Erin said, "Throw in a little kleptomania, and you've got it."

Despite her light tone, I could hear the anguish underneath. I told her, "When your father goes into treatment, you'll all be involved in family counseling. That's going to open some doors."

"Just keep saying 'when,' " Erin said, "not 'if.' "

Moira pulled over to the curb, and I stopped in back of her. There wasn't any other car nearby that might be Axel's. Erin noticed that too, and asked candidly, "How much were you counting on Axel?"

"Doing what I do," I said, "I've learned not to count on anyone."

A few minutes later, I wondered if I'd made an error in not having asked someone about the physical layout of the O'Brien place. We had to walk up a flight of steps directly off the street, then a long uphill expanse of yard, followed by another long steep stairway to get to the deck in front of the house. By the time we'd reached the top, the climb plus our anxiety about going in had left us weak and breathless. Charles looked even more haggard than earlier, and Pixie's euphoric mood had now plummeted into depression.

I would have liked to stay on the deck a few minutes to let everyone recover, but Adele opened the front door and urgently beckoned us into the entrance hallway. She spoke in a hushed, stricken voice. "Axel called. He missed his plane—he's going to catch the next flight, but he could be as much as an hour late."

I could tell from the look in her eyes that she'd been counting heavily on Jed's boss's presence and was now condemning herself for having instigated the intervention—and if there had been any way for her to call it off, she would have. It's a familiar phenomenon in intervention called "buyer's remorse."

I glanced at my watch. It was 9:25. No telling whether Axel

would arrive in time to be of help. But an intervention is a little like a rocket launch. Once you begin, you can't turn back. When unexpected circumstances arise to prevent people from being on time or even coming at all, I cope. So I assured them, "We're going to go right ahead, gang. No turning back. This is it."

"I'm with you," Erin said.

"Everybody else, too? Well?"

"Of course," Moira said.

I wondered where Jed was. Standing in the entrance hall, I could see into an open kitchen area on my left. To the right was a dining area with a brick-hearthed fireplace.

We all followed Adele through the dining area into a long narrow living room with bay windows at the far end looking out over the ocean. Adele grimly offered us coffee from an urn on a low table. She said Jed was down in the laundry room and would be coming upstairs any minute. Behind the fireplace, I'd noticed steps descending to the lower level.

I knew from things that had been said at the preparation that when Jed went to the laundry room, he didn't run down to do a load of wash. But when Pixie made a disparaging remark about her father's stash, I reminded her sternly that she wasn't to say anything to Jed. Ignoring the hurt look in her eyes, I told everyone where I wanted him or her to sit. Then I positioned myself on the arm of the couch nearest the top of the stairway, where I could intercept Jed.

I didn't have long to wait before I heard his footsteps.

Halfway up, he saw me and stopped. Even in the dim light of the stairwell, I could tell the year since I'd seen him had taken its toll. His face was puffy, his eyes bleared.

I smiled and said, "Hello, Jed."

There was a thick beat of silence, but his expression didn't reveal a flicker of emotion as he said, "I remember you. You're Ed Storti."

"That's right. It's good to see you again."

That earned me a chilly half-smile.

I went on quickly, "Jed, I'm sure you know why I'm here. I want to talk to you about your drinking."

"Who's with you?" And he was up the steps and past me, not pushing me aside exactly, but something close to that. He stopped on the top step, stood with his left hand curled just a little regally around the pillar of the balustrade, and looked into the living room.

Adele, too nervous to remain seated, had gone to stand at the far end of the living room. She avoided looking at Jed, and I think if I had told her then she didn't have to be there, she would have left.

Erin and Moira were seated side by side on a small loveseat. Their expressions were strained yet resolute as they faced their father. Charles sat across from them staring down at the cup of coffee he was holding. He looked miserable.

Pixie was huddled in the deep wing chair I'd told her to sit in, and I couldn't see her face.

I moved past Jed to resume my half-standing, half-sitting position on the arm of the couch, which put me in a strong mediating posture—able to call on the people behind me, or stand and face Jed without seeming obtrusive.

Jed said, "I'm going to get a cup of coffee," in a tone that dismissed everyone.

I said, "Good. Then we can settle down and talk about why your family wants you to get help."

I doubted he would come among us to get his coffee from the urn on the table, and I was right. We all watched in silence as he went into the kitchen, poured himself a cup from the pot on the countertop, then put it in the microwave. Waiting for it to heat, he smiled in at us coolly.

Reacting, Adele nervously brushed a strand of hair away from her forehead.

Jed took his coffee cup out of the microwave and again went to stand next to the balustrade. In a slightly patronizing tone he said, "Look, Ed, I know what you do. We can skip the preliminaries. Just tell me the bottom line."

I said, "Jed, I get the feeling you don't know how truly ill you are."

His eyes moved slowly and coldly from my toes to my head as though he were analyzing my components on a computer screen. I sensed it was a look he used often in negotiating sessions. He said, "When I came up those stairs just now, I was on my way to go for a five-mile run on the beach—which, by the way, I do every damn morning. So don't tell me I'm ill."

I said, "I ran when I was drinking, Jed. So do animals trapped in mazes. It's treadmill behavior, easier to do than standing still and facing the truth."

"I'm not a drunk. I can handle my drinking. I always have and always will. And you'd better understand, I'm not negotiating a thing with you, because there's nothing at stake here."

I had to build a foundation with Jed. So I said, "Your life is. It's so obvious your health is breaking down. Your face is swollen. I see broken blood vessels in your face. You have bloodshot eyes. You come home at night and you're unconscious by eight o'clock. If anybody asked you what happened between walking into your house and going to bed, you probably wouldn't be able to tell them. We're not going to allow you to die like this. You're too good a man."

His deep frown was one of anger, not worry about anything I was saying. "I'm tired when I get home. I go to bed."

"You don't sleep, you pass out. Your family is frightened for you."

"Yeah, well, I'll make a deal with my family here and now. If they stay out of my life, I'll stay out of theirs."

"Jed, you don't mean that. Look at them—the love is still there. They're terrified about what's happening to you, yet no matter how many times they tell you, you don't listen."

"I can't help what they worry about," he said flatly.

We were sparring too much. As depleted as he was, Jed's debating skills were so deeply ingrained that using them was almost automatic, and he was treating our encounter as though it were a strike negotiation. I wanted to call on someone to reinforce the things I was telling him and also reach him on a feeling level. I had two choices.

A glance at Moira told me her anxiety level was still way too high.

Erin's forthright expression as her eyes met mine told me she'd try.

I said, "Erin?"

Her eyes sought his. "You've always been my 'lion' poppa, Dad. No matter how scary the world got, you were there. Remember when I was in junior high and we were sitting on the beach and I told you I wanted to try some marijuana and had some joints in my purse. You didn't say a word, you just opened my purse, took out the cigarettes, swam out in the ocean with them, came back, told me you'd 'drowned' them. Well, I'd like to drown all the whiskey you drink. Because everything Ed has told you is true. You look awful. I'm not ever going to stop loving you, but to know you could get better and having to watch you get worse . . . well, it's getting harder and harder for me to come and visit."

What she'd said obviously moved Jed, but not enough. "I am just not in the bad shape you all think I am," he said.

I was readying my next onslaught when the doorbell rang.

Adele left the room, and Jed's eyes followed her. A moment later, she returned with Axel. I felt a surge of energy when I saw him, knew everyone in the room felt it, too. That's one advantage a late arrival can give an intervention—it's like an infusion of new blood.

But Jed was furious. "Christ, Axel, what the hell are you doing here?"

"I'm late," Axel said simply.

Moving forward to draw him into the living room, I saw he was a whip-thin man with brown hair silvering at the temples.

His handshake confirmed the feeling I'd had that he would be a strong ally, able to say the things we'd talked about on the phone.

I said, "Axel, we've been discussing Jed's drinking problem and the effect it's having on his life."

Axel nodded.

"I still don't understand why *you're* here," Jed repeated. "There's a strike going on up north."

"I'm here for two reasons. One, I'm your friend, and two, you work for me."

"Jed, you must know your drinking is affecting your work," I said.

He was furious. "Don't pull that! Work is one place I always function."

Axel shook his head. "You're just not doing the job any more, and your credibility is shot."

"That's crap! I—"

But Axel didn't let him in. "When you sign a memo, people ask me if you signed it in the morning or the afternoon so they can gauge how to take it. They figure at ten o'clock, you've had a pint, and by two o'clock, a fifth. Anything you write after noon, they ignore."

During the ten seconds it took Axel to say that—partly because he'd said it in front of Jed's family—Jed's confidence crumbled. His expression became naked, vulnerable.

I'd witnessed that happening other times—people withstanding pleas by their families and friends, cracking when their job performance was exposed.

"Axel is telling you the truth, Jed. That's why you need to enter a treatment center today and start putting your disease in remission."

I had to stay focused on his entering a treatment center immediately, because he'd resist that more than anything, even more than admitting his drinking problem.

"I'll give up the booze," he stated. "I've stopped before, so I know I can do it. This time I'll stop for good."

I answered, "But to succeed, you and your family need the help of a treatment center."

"The hell with it! If my family wants help, I'll hire the best damned psychiatrist I can find. But *I* can quit alone!"

"Not this time. You need support. I've made arrangements at an excellent center."

"The hell you have!"

"In fact," I continued calmly, "it's the same place your colleague Bob went."

"You want me to go in as an outpatient?"

"No, as an inpatient."

He protested. "Why as inpatient? Bob was completely out of it. I'm not."

"Jed," Axel said softly, "you missed the last council meeting."

Jed's eyes had a trapped expression. "Christ," he muttered under his breath. Then, "How long would I have to be in there?"

"A few weeks."

"I can't be away from the office that long."

I looked at Axel.

"Yes, you can. We'll cover you. The time isn't important."

Jed held up a hand defensively. "I promise I'll go to an outpatient center today. I'll call right now. Jesus, you can watch me make the call."

His eyes pleaded with Axel, who said, "How many years have you been drinking? Thirty? An outpatient center isn't going to be enough. I *know* you. If you go to an outpatient center at night, you'll be drinking all day."

I said, "More than just getting off alcohol, you have to repair the damage that's been done to your body and learn to understand the nature of the disease you have."

Jed was silent, still seeking that escape hatch. "Next week is Thanksgiving . . . the holidays. I'll go in after Christmas."

Moira was looking more confident now. I called on her.

She said, "*Now,* Dad. You getting better is all we want this Christmas." Her eyes held her father's. "Will you give us that?"

Jed's head went down. I believed we had him and this exhausted, desperately ill man was going to accept help.

Without looking up, he said, "I want to go for my run." He phrased it as a statement—and yet his tone of voice asked if I would accept his doing that.

It summoned a memory of the running I did when I was drinking, and what a self-confronting time it was. The entire run, I would ask myself, "Why do you drink, Ed?"

At this moment, Jed needed to run because routine would get him through what was happening. I'd have wanted that myself.

I asked, "How long does your run usually take?"

He gave a shake of his shoulders. "Today—not too long."

"And when you get back?"

"A shower."

"Then?" I waited.

"I'll go with you."

I couldn't hold back the grin. "Go for your run."

While Jed was running, there was a lot of laughter and talking in the O'Brien living room between Moira and Erin, Axel and Adele. Adele's tense expression and pallor were gone and she looked ten years younger.

Charles didn't enter in. Nor did Pixie, who had left the shelter of the wing chair and now stood at the far end of the room looking out the window. What was she watching? I wondered. Something only she could see?

I felt it was important to draw everyone together while we waited for Jed to return, so I started describing the outpatient counseling sessions Adele and the children would be participating in. I intentionally directed questions to both Charles and Pixie, wanting to draw them into the group. Charles responded in monosyllables, but Pixie remained with her back to us until I tried again. Then she turned, her hands clasped into fists. She cried, "Just leave me alone and out of it! Is that clear?" She ran toward the stairs.

"Pixie?"

Erin reached out, but Pixie pushed past her sister, racing down the stairway.

A second later, we heard more footsteps, Jed's, coming up to the deck outside. When he entered the house, he went directly into the kitchen, picked up the phone, and dialed. "Helen? I want you to cancel my appointments for the coming month." He glanced at us. "I'm going into an alcohol treatment center today. Yes, you can tell anybody who wants to know where I am."

Twenty minutes later, he had showered and packed and was ready to leave.

The original plan had been for everyone to go to the treatment center with Jed. But when Adele called downstairs to Pixie, there was no response.

"I'll stay with her," Erin said.

Driving to the center, I kept thinking about Pixie, knowing she was far from all right.

When we arrived at the center, I stayed at the admissions desk with Axel, helping him complete the forms while Adele and Moira went to help Jed get settled in his room.

When Axel and I went up to say goodbye, Jed was demanding to know why he couldn't read the magazines he'd brought.

"The only things you're going to read during the next few weeks will be focused on what you need to do to get well," the counselor said firmly.

Still deeply concerned about Pixie, I asked the counselor if I could use the phone in his office. He nodded, and I went in and called the O'Brien house. There was no answer.

Because I was troubled about Pixie and also because I had undertaken an intervention in a family with so many serious problems, I kept in close touch with them in the weeks immediately following Jed's entering treatment.

Adele told me that she, Moira, Erin, and even Charles were participating intensely in the family counseling sessions.

I asked about Pixie, and she said Pixie would join the counseling sessions as soon as her school's winter recess began.

It was obvious to me that Adele was so euphoric about Jed's getting the help he needed, she wasn't really focusing on her youngest daughter's problems.

Erin confirmed that. Deeply concerned about Pixie, she kept trying to talk to her, but Pixie evaded her, and Erin had the impression her sister was close to a breakdown.

I urged her to try to get Pixie to come talk to me.

On Christmas Eve, Erin called, half laughing, half crying, to tell me Pixie had admitted herself into the eating-disorders unit at the same treatment center where Jed was.

I called the head counselor of the unit, and he told me how truly ill she was. Her bulimia, excessive drinking, and pot smoking had all damaged her system, and she was going to be under close medical supervision for several days. I asked him to call me as soon as she was stable. The day he did, I went to see her, and we had our first long talk with the barriers down. She described in detail what she'd been going through before my intervention with Jed.

She said, "The morning of the intervention, I felt like there were searchlights hidden all over the house; maybe one of the search beams would land on me and someone would shout, 'What about *your* problem, Pixie?' I just wanted the intervention to be over so I could have some beer and smoke a joint I had stashed away. Then when you started talking about the family counseling we all had to go to, I panicked. I knew I couldn't sit through any of that without falling apart.

"Mom thought I was in school the week the counseling started, but I stayed home that whole time. With her visiting

Dad every day at the hospital, I was alone most of the time. What a routine. I would get my beer and books and drink the beer and never open a book."

She related how one morning she'd found a brochure Adele had brought home about the different kinds of problems the hospital dealt with: alcohol, drugs, eating disorders. She said reading it upset her, because she had all those problems. She was hiding her booze in the house just as Jed had. She'd reached the point where every time she ate, she vomited whether she wanted to or not.

Reading the brochure made her suddenly want to take care of everything that was hanging over her. That afternoon, she drove into San Pedro to pay some parking tickets. After doing that, she realized her life was filled with too many problems she couldn't cope with or resolve.

She went back home, straightened up her room, and put on her running clothes. By then it was night. At first she ran along her dad's route, then she started cutting through backyards, and finally she was on the Pacific Coast Highway. She ran all the way into San Pedro and up a steep hill to the hospital, just running and running. She circled through the trees until she came to the unit Jed was in and started looking in the windows. She said, "I didn't really expect to see him, but there he was, sitting on top of a table leading a discussion group. He looked . . . not happy, but involved. I knew he'd do okay if they let him be in charge of something."

After the meeting ended, Jed and the others left and somebody turned out the lights. Pixie stood staring at the dark windows, deciding whether to stay outside alone or go in where there were people.

Finally she went around to the front door and walked in.

She was put in the eating-disorders unit—which was right across the hall from Jed's unit.

She said, "I thought Dad would be furious with me for making such a mess of myself, so every time I saw him coming down the corridor, I'd run into another room.

59

"One of my buddies from high school was admitted into my dad's alcohol/drug group. Dad told Tim, 'Tim, if you see Pixie, try to get her to stop hiding from me.'

"Tim was someone I could hug and talk to. One day when he came to me and said, 'Come on, Pixie, let's go see your dad,' I started crying. Pretty soon I got hysterical. It was strange, like poison was rushing out of me through my tears. But Tim stayed right there, holding me until I calmed down.

"Then I went to see my dad."

I went to talk with Jed that afternoon, too, and he told me how hard it had been having Pixie admit herself while he was in treatment. He said her doing that threw him into a bucket of feelings he wasn't prepared to deal with. "I thought, 'God, I can cope with this for myself, but I can't cope with it for my daughter.' The realization of what it could mean for someone that young—well, I took it very hard."

The counselor in Jed's unit told me Jed had had no true idea how Pixie had felt about him, the closeness she was looking for. When he did begin to understand it through counseling, it was difficult for him to accept. It was his style to watch his children from afar, be protective and provide for them, but at the same time, not get intimate.

As difficult and frightening as it was for Jed to change, to learn how to be open for the first time, he started working on it.

A few months after he left the aftercare program, he received another jolt when Charles declared himself an alcoholic. But Jed was stronger then and able to offer a great deal of help and support to his son.

The last time I saw Jed, he told me he was still working on finding ways to express his feelings and probably always would be.

I think it's because Jed's intervention was done so close to the holidays and Pixie admitted herself into treatment on Christmas Eve that all the O'Briens send me cards and notes at Christmastime.

Last Christmas, two years after she and her father entered treatment, Pixie wrote: "Little things make me feel good these days, small disciplines. I'm going to art school. I was lying in bed this morning, thinking, I don't want to drive all the way to school because I know we're not going to do anything important.

"Then I thought, Wait a minute. You never know what you might come up with—like maybe a new fabric design. So I got up and went to school. That's what I mean, one small discipline—or challenge—at a time. They're piling up, too, growing, building something, and so am I."

It's always hard for parents to accept a child's addiction. Many go through the same stages bereaved parents do—denial and isolation, anger and guilt, bargaining, depression—before they reach acceptance. And sometimes they prolong the negative stages for years of heartache and pain before they finally act.

Doctors, lawyers, and psychoanalysts have "classic" cases they remember and refer to over and over again.

Sarah and Julian Knight are my classic parents who endured too much, too long.

Sarah, Julian, and Ben

I met Sarah and Julian Knight a year before I actually intervened with their son.

Ira Levine, a psychotherapist who worked effectively with chemical-dependent teenagers, called and asked if I could come and talk to the Knights at St. Monica's Hospital in Los Angeles, where their son Ben had been admitted to the emergency room after overdosing on cocaine.

I'm often asked to meet with parents in hospital settings. I find it appalling that at this point in time when mortality and morbidity rates are declining steadily for all segments of the population, the incidence of death and illness among forty million American adolescents is 11 percent higher than it was ten years ago and that substance abuse is recognized as a leading contributing factor.

When I arrived at the hospital, Ira took me into the counselor's office to tell me about Ben Knight's critical life circumstances. He described Ben as an athletically gifted, articulate seventeen-year-old with an IQ of 140+. From early childhood on, the boy had been outstanding in all sports, and in his first year in high school he had been named all-city shortstop. But in the middle of his sophomore year, he began getting low grades, became frequently truant, and was put on probation for possession of marijuana on campus. When that happened, Ben's parents persuaded him to enter psychotherapy with Ira, and it was then Ira discovered Ben had been excessively using drugs for years. He'd started smoking pot in sixth grade, then went on to experiment with amphetamines, speed, cocaine, and heroin—though alcohol and marijuana remained his drugs of choice.

It was a depressingly familiar story. A lot of adolescents who decide to experiment with drugs start out with marijuana. Their peers who are already using it convince them it's nonaddictive and safe. In fact, its mildly hallucinogenic properties alter perceptions of distance, dimension, and time, and impair short-term memory, concentration, coordination, and judgment. Also, marijuana contains more than 400 chemicals. At least sixty have long-term effects on the mind and/or behavior. THC (delta-9-tetrahydrocannabinol), the primary psychoactive component, is a fat-soluble substance absorbed by the body's fatty tissues, and even when released, may be reabsorbed in the intestines and recycled. So a week or even longer after someone has smoked a joint, a fourth to a third of the THC can still be present.

Even the staunchest advocates of cannabis agree that using marijuana in the teen years inhibits the maturation process. And yet, in the past three decades, it has become, next to alcohol, the favorite drug of American youth. In 1962, only

1 percent of young people aged twelve to seventeen had ever tried it. But through its association with the counterculture movement of the mid-'60s, that figure rose dramatically and continued to rise in the '70s and '80s.

Some teenagers use marijuana a few times and stop. Others keep using it intermittently on into adulthood, unaware of its subtle cumulative effect on their biochemistry. But addiction-prone teenagers quickly become psychologically dependent on it, want it every day. As Dr. Mitchell S. Rosenthal of Phoenix House put it, "At a time when [they] should be developing long-range goals, their time frame is shrinking. When they most need to learn how to deal responsibly with others, they become more self-involved, more infantile. Instead of expanding, their world is contracting. Rather than cope with pressures, they escape them. They do not cope, and they do not learn how to cope. They do not grow up, and some may never grow up."

And many—like Ben Knight—are encouraged by their "success" with marijuana to experiment with other, harder substances.

When I asked Ira why so many years passed before anything was done about Ben's excessive drug use, he said there were two reasons. First, Ben had always been able to convince people he didn't have a drug problem.

Unfortunately, many addictive individuals learn at an early age how to manipulate parents and siblings into believing nothing is seriously wrong even when they're having such major problems with stress that they've already begun seeking chemical relief. Eventually, reversal takes place; the chemical creates the stress. By adolescence, they're able to convince the most observant and intuitive people they're not chemical-dependent. Then as young adults they're primed to click right into relationships they can control until their manipulation becomes so refined it seems almost automatic. Too often it takes a disaster—the operation botched by a surgeon high on cocaine, the tragic car crash caused by a drunk, or an addict's fatal overdose—to expose addiction's power over all its victims—those who are addicted and those who are affected by the addicted person's actions.

The second reason so much time passed without anything being done, Ira went on, was Ben's father. He explained that Julian Knight was the chairman of the philosophy department at a nearby university—which, Ira said, was a bit like having Plato for a father. As a philosopher, Julian's belief system was based on rationality and logic. Over the years, he had tried to "reason" Ben away from using drugs, and though he hadn't succeeded, he remained convinced that ultimately he would be able to reach his son.

"I would have asked you to intervene with Ben when I started working with him," Ira said, "but Julian was opposed to it. Even after what's happened today, you may have trouble convincing him that Ben should go straight from the hospital into treatment."

On my way down to the waiting room to talk to the Knights, I stopped in the emergency room to see Ben. A nurse pointed to a bed with a portable curtain drawn around it. I drew it partly open.

Ben was still unconscious. An intravenous solution dripped down from a plastic bag and through a tube into his arm. He was a handsome kid, but pale and exhausted-looking, with the tension lines aging his features I see in many teenagers who are old in their addiction.

I glanced at the chart clipped to his bed.

There are three stages to a cocaine reaction. All affect the body's respiratory, cardiovascular, and central nervous systems. In the early phase, there is a sudden headache, nausea, vomiting, twitching of fingers and toes, a rise in body temperature, increased breathing and pulse rate, and elevated blood pressure. In the second phase, there are convulsions, loss of urine and bowel control, and irregular breathing, heartbeat, and pulse, and the skin turns blue. In the final phase, there is paralysis, coma, loss of reflexes, fluid in the lungs, and breathing failure, until the heart finally stops.

Ben had had a phase-two reaction. His vital signs were good and he was going to recover—but if his friends had waited a little longer before calling for help, he would be dead now.

I left him and went to the hospital waiting room to meet Sarah and Julian Knight.

Julian was a tall, lanky man with a high forehead above gray eyes. His voice was so soft I had to incline my head toward him when he was speaking, and there was a gentle cadence to his speech I couldn't place until he mentioned he was from Kentucky.

Sarah Knight was a small, guarded woman with a quickness to her movements and bright brown eyes. She sat on the vinyl couch next to her husband, her hands pulling at the purse strap in her lap.

Both listened intently as I said I believed their son should enter a treatment center as soon as he was well enough to leave the hospital. Then I described the intervention process. I stated that Ben had OD'd, and the shock of that *should* be sufficient to get him to admit the damage addiction was inflicting on his own life, but it probably wouldn't. Addictive individuals will blame people, circumstances, or anything else before they will blame anything remotely connected to the substance they're addicted to. "That's why we need to create a positive crisis to help him face the reality of his disease," I said.

When I'd finished, Julian seemed uneasy. I asked what he was thinking.

"I just don't understand how things have gotten this bad for Ben. Driving here this afternoon, I started thinking about the summers we used to spend on my folks' farm when Ben was small. He loved those summers. There was something about Kentucky, the fishing and hunting, the land, the people, that seemed to touch him on a deep level. Maybe if he'd grown up there instead of . . ." His voice trailed off. He shook his head. "No. Even then, there were signs something was wrong. One summer, I remember, he'd been reading *Tom Sawyer*. He was so fascinated with the part where Tom and Huck ran away, then went back and eavesdropped on their own funeral, he decided to try it himself. He packed a knapsack and set out one evening. There was a storm, and when he didn't come home, I went out looking for him. The rain was pelting down, the lightning zagging across the hills. I met him coming through the gate, wet and scared, and he told me what he'd planned.

"I've wondered so often—why did he want to hear what the rest of his family would say about him if we thought he were dead?" He stood up, walked to the window, stood staring out.

I thought how early Ben must have started exhibiting addictive traits—many of which I'd experienced in my own childhood: feelings of isolation and perceptions so acute they made the world seem a painful place to be. Often such traits surface as early as age six or eight, and when you talk to chemical-dependent teenagers, many of them will say things like "Yeah, sometimes I felt like an alien, or I'd been adopted and didn't really belong to my family," or "I had so many problems as a little kid I could hardly wait to grow up because I figured then they'd all go away."

Sarah said softly, "Ben's always been able to mix us up. He'd do something that would convince me he'd never get his life straightened out—and then, two hours later, come up and give me a big hug, and I'd think, 'It's all right, he's going to be okay.'

"For a long time I've been telling myself, well, we're not as badly off as some other families. Ben isn't in jail like so-and-so. But this afternoon, he almost died. Now I realize I should have been asking myself what was *wrong*."

She turned to Julian. "Remember how . . ." But her voice trailed off.

"Remember what?" I asked.

"Julian took Ben on a canoe trip into the Canadian Rockies last summer. He was convinced Ben would come back"—a tired smile softened her tenseness for a moment—"better."

Julian turned to face us and said, "He *was* better on that trip. He was full of zest and energy, ready to take risks, just as he'd been as a kid. I pushed us both to the limit, maybe even a little beyond. There were a couple of times in white water I was terrified, and I know Ben was, too. But I wanted him to find out all the good stuff he had inside. I think he did. Yet a week after we got back, he was drinking and using as heavily as before."

"His disease is that powerful," I said.

"Disease?" he echoed in a baffled tone.

I talked to him about the disease of addiction, explaining its major symptoms: unpredictability, buildup of tolerance to alcohol and drugs, physical deterioration, blackouts, social withdrawal. I told him, "I'm not surprised Ben was attracted to that episode in *Tom Sawyer*. Mark Twain had an addictive personality, went through bouts of despair and pessimism, married a frail woman he could control, was obsessed by gambling. As a writer, he invested many of his characters with addictive traits."

I went on to discuss the cyclic pattern of addictive behavior; how, in the early stages, a chemical-dependent person could have six good days to one bad, but gradually, the good ones dwindled and the ratio became five good to one bad, then four to one, three to one, two to one. Yet people close to the addicted person are always lured by the good days until their own responsive behavior mirrors the cycle of the disease. On bad days, family and friends might reach a point where they become convinced they can't take it anymore. Then when the behavior of the person swings back and becomes "tolerable," they relapse into hopefulness and open themselves to participate in the next crisis.

So just as addicted people don't want to face their disease, people close to them, instead of helping them face it, make excuse-chains to explain away truancies from school, absenteeism from jobs, broken appointments. If the addicted person does manage to fulfill some obligation, family members want so much to believe everything is going to be fine from then on, they convince themselves it will be.

Yet even as I was telling him these things, Julian's equivocal expression was making me fear he was going to try to find a philosophical explanation for what Ben was going through.

I quickly asked both Knights if their parents or grandparents had had problems with alcohol, because becoming chemical-dependent at an early age, as Ben had, was a prime indicator his disease had a genetic foundation.

Sarah said her father, a career officer in the army, had been a heavy drinker while in the service, but after being given a medical account of the disastrous things drinking was doing to his health, had stopped "cold-turkey" and now didn't drink at all.

Julian acknowledged his own grandfather hadn't gone a day without his moonshine.

I told them about the genetic component of the disease and said, "I've worked with a lot of young people who 'inherited' addiction, and I can tell you this: because of their biochemical and psychological makeup, they respond to and crave chemical relief in a way people without this disease just don't understand. And even though I've never met Ben, I can tell you pretty much what his behavior has been like."

Julian looked skeptical but he said, "Go ahead."

I gave him the profile of an addicted teenager: the denial, self-delusion, excessive need for privacy, shyness, defiance, lack of self-discipline, erratic eating, plummeting grades, boredom and lethargy, Jekyll/Hyde unpredictability.

Julian's expression acknowledged the accuracy of my description, but he asked, "Can't those things also be attributed to the sheer emotional burdens of adolescence—trying to be attractive, trying to make it with girls, trying to be an athletic star, and being inundated on all sides with the image of the hard-drinking society we live in, on television, even the local drag strip? Once I think it might have been the exception to behave as Ben is. Now I don't believe it is."

I said, "How many other young people do you know who have overdosed?"

He didn't answer.

I pushed on. "The point is, a chemical is the common denominator in Ben's life. You must be able to see by now there is a deteriorating pattern to Ben's behavior. Probably things he was doing that once concerned you, you've put out of your mind, because other, bigger problems are surfacing. Like what happened today."

Frowning deeply, Julian asked, "What can intervention do to combat the things you've described?"

I said, "Through intervention, we can motivate Ben to enter a treatment center, where he'll begin facing his addiction and receive guidance on making intelligent choices about how to live the rest of his life. He can't do that alone."

Both Knights were thoughtful, quiet for several moments. I sensed Sarah was ready to intervene right now. So I was dismayed when Julian said, "I believe what happened today will have a profound effect on Ben. I really would prefer it, and I think Ben would be better off, if he could reach the decision to stop drinking, stop taking drugs, on his own."

"He can't," I said firmly, and I wanted to say more, but a nurse came to the waiting room to tell the Knights Ben had regained consciousness and was asking for them. Julian shook my hand and said in a tone of courteous finality. "I appreciate your coming, Mr. Storti. But I'm convinced I'm doing the right thing."

Sarah's eyes met mine, and I sensed she didn't agree with Julian. But she remained silent.

Driving home that evening, I was filled with frustration, wondering what I could have said or done to convince the Knights their son needed immediate help. Episodes I'd gone through with other parents who had refused to act against their children's addiction began to fill my mind—and inevitably, because I was wrestling with a sense of failure, my thoughts settled on one of the bleakest: Paul and Eric Strader. I wondered if what had happened to Eric would one day have to happen to Ben.

Paul Strader and I had been longshoremen together. After I left the waterfront, he'd gone on to become a dock foreman. He was a man who took intense pride in the externals of his life. His home always looked freshly painted, the windows gleamed, the yard was beautifully kept. All his children were high achievers—except for Eric.

The afternoon Paul called me, his usually jaunty voice was subdued. "Eric's in jail, Ed. Second arrest for possession of a controlled substance."

"I'm sorry, Paul," I said, knowing the second arrest for possession was a felony, but not surprised to hear about the arrest. Eric had been involved in petty crimes in junior high and progressively more serious ones as he grew older. Now he was an apprentice longshoreman and, according to waterfront rumor, spent every cent he earned on heroin. Paul had depleted his savings to bail his son out of one scrape after another, depriving himself and his wife, Mary, of things like a long-planned trip to Hawaii they'd canceled in order to pay for a car Eric had wrecked. When parents accept negative behavior or excessive drug use by their children, it's almost inevitable that their own lives become unmanageable. And I believed every time Paul "rescued" Eric instead of dealing with the addiction, he was telling his son, in effect, "You don't have to solve your problems, I'll solve them for you." As the number of bail-outs mounted, Eric got the message he would have an unlimited number of second chances.

Remembering Paul's pattern with Eric, I wondered what Julian and Sarah had given up to pay for that canoe trip into the Canadian wilderness, how many other "Save Ben" enterprises they'd undertaken trying to circumvent his addiction when what they needed to do was confront it.

I'd asked Paul that day, "How can I help?"

He told me the public defender had said if he could get Eric into an extended inpatient treatment program, it was possible the judge would waive his sentence.

It was another rescue attempt on Paul's part, but one that would also require work and commitment from Eric. Knowing what a positive step it could be for Eric and the whole Strader family if we could get Eric into treatment, I said, "I'd have to assess him before asking a center to accept him."

"I know," Paul replied. "I was hoping you might be able to drive down to the jail with me this afternoon, talk to him, see what you think. His sentencing will be at the end of the week, so we have to have a place that will accept him by then."

An hour later, I was sitting opposite Eric in the visiting room at the county holding facility. Looking at him through the plastic screen that separated us inside the wooden cubicle, I realized I wouldn't have recognized him if I'd passed him on the street. Paul had mentioned that Eric was thirty-one but he looked as if he were in his forties.

I told him if he agreed to enter an inpatient treatment facility for a sixty-to-ninety-day period we might be able to get his sentence waived and keep it waived, depending upon reports about his progress. But I also told him how hard he would have to work to succeed.

At the end of our conversation, I didn't get the feeling he was ready to face his disease, nor did I think he had any real awareness of the pain his addiction was inflicting on Paul. He agreed to enter treatment because it would keep him out of prison.

When our time in the cubicle was up, Paul quickly asked Eric if he needed anything, and Eric asked for money.

At the exit door, Paul handed twenty dollars to the bailiff, saying, "For Eric Strader."

I knew dope was available in that facility, and I doubted Eric wanted the money for toothpaste.

As we were driving away from the facility, I said, "Paul, I think you and Mary should consider getting counseling or going to ALANON so you can become aware of the enabling you're doing. Giving Eric twenty dollars just now was *not* a good idea."

Paul's hands tightened on the steering wheel. "I can't seem to help it."

Many people I work with are so enmeshed in the disease of addiction, they don't even hear me when I suggest avenues of help. I knew Paul hadn't. He and his wife were as addicted to Eric as Eric was to heroin.

When I called him later that week to tell him I'd found a treatment center in northern California that had agreed to accept Eric, his first reaction was, "That's kind of far away. To visit him, I mean."

I said firmly, "He has too many drug connections here. It will be best to get Eric out of the Long Beach area." I was tempted to add, "And far enough away from his family so he has to rely on himself."

After a moment of silence Paul said, "You're right. I'm just scared to let go."

And he didn't.

The treatment center I'd found for Eric was a stark, no-nonsense facility with an impressive recovery rate among hard-core users. Paul made weekly trips to northern California to visit and supply Eric with extra spending money, clothes, incidentals. But neither he nor his wife attended any of the family counseling sessions.

A few weeks into the program, Eric used some of the spending money Paul gave him to buy drugs, and was discharged from the program. Since he had defied his probation agreement, he was sent to prison.

It seemed to me Ben Knight was heading down the same road. At seventeen, he'd given up on his outstanding athletic potential and his chances of going to college, he'd lost good friends, he'd had minor scrapes with the law, and he was inflicting pain on his family as insensibly as Eric had his. My concerns about Ben eddied into the same bleak corner of my mind as my memories of Eric. I doubted I'd ever see Ben again.

But almost a year to the day after my meeting them at the hospital, Ira Levine called me again about the Knights. He said the family had been dealt another blow: Julian Knight had been diagnosed as having pancreatic cancer. Sarah had been displacing her grief and anxiety over her husband's illness by coming down hard on Ben. She'd ordered the boy to stop smoking pot and drinking and get his grades up enough to graduate, viewing his graduation as a perhaps final gift he could give his father.

"Predictably," Ira said, "as attention and energy once focused on coping with Ben's problems has shifted to Julian's cancer, Ben's gotten worse. And people he might have confided in in the past—his dad, his sister, a coach he was fond of, me—he won't even talk to. He's blanking us out. I think he's saying to himself, 'I have to give up on them before they give up on me.' And every day, he moves a little closer to the edge.

"Sarah is ready for you to intervene right now. Julian isn't, but he knows his wife is going through hell, and maybe that will carry some weight. Would you talk to them again?"

I said that of course I would.

After a moment's hesitation, Ira said, "Ed, you'd better know, if you do get Julian's consent to intervene, Ben's pattern, when he can't con people, is to bolt. I'm not certain he'll stand still for an intervention."

I replied that unfortunately was true of a lot of addicted young people. Far more teenagers run from interventions than adults. Adolescents think they have ninety-nine lives left, and nothing tragic can happen to them; or, if it does, they'll survive.

Ira gave me Sarah Knight's phone number and I said I'd call her right away.

She answered on the first ring, said she'd been waiting for my call. I could tell from her almost frantic answers to my questions she was in pain.

She said, "I knew the day we spoke to you at the hospital we should have intervened. Julian's willing to talk to you again. How soon can you see us?"

We set up a meeting at my office the next morning. I didn't say so, but in addition to talking to Julian again, I wanted to assess Sarah. Between her husband's illness and Ben's addiction, she'd been under so much stress, I needed to be certain she'd be strong enough to take part in an intervention and accept its outcome.

The sun was shining brightly as I drove to the office the next morning, but the air was cool and there were clouds around the edge of the sky that meant a storm was probably on the way.

The Knights arrived at 9:45. I thought Julian looked frailer than he had a year ago; Sarah stronger.

They sat down on the couch, accepted my offer of coffee. Then I asked what had been going on with Ben during the past year.

Sarah answered. "He was placed on probation from school again. He's been arrested twice for public drunkenness. He's been in fights, lost his two front teeth. He's had two car accidents. There's more." She gave a nervous laugh. "The crazy thing is, if Julian didn't have cancer, I guess we'd still be putting up with all this. Now I just won't. I want him to get help, or I want him out of our lives." Her voice was defensive.

"Sarah," Julian said softly.

She shook her head. "No. I mean it. Out."

Looking at me, Julian said softly. "I've been hoping my illness would interact with Ben's addiction in a positive way. I told myself I'd bear whatever burdens had been placed upon me, believing or at least wanting to believe my suffering would be redeeming for Ben, that it would help him assume some responsibility. And there have been days, sort of oases in his behavior, when I thought it was. But . . ." He shook his head. "You always want to believe what you don't want to see isn't there."

The tone of his voice was desolate, and Sarah reached out quickly to touch his hand, saying, "It isn't that Ben doesn't care about what's happening to Julian. I know he does. I can tell from the questions he asks. Ben just can't face problems. When we found out Julian had cancer, I set up a family meeting with Ira Levine and Ben's counselor at school so we could all talk about it, deal with our feelings. Ben ran away from that meeting, and I realized then that he's been running his whole life."

My eyes met Sarah's, and I intuited what she was thinking: How can you convince this critically ill man, no matter how much philosophical understanding he offers, Ben can't use it to heal himself?

I said, "I can't think of a harder situation for a boy like Ben to be in than to know you're ill and that he's behaving the opposite of the way he should be behaving."

"Then why is he?" Julian asked in a despairing tone.

"Because he's ill," I said. "Julian, just as your cells, without any warning, mutated into cancerous ones, Ben's disease, too, is a function of biochemistry and the failure of his immune system. You must understand Ben's addiction isn't due to weakness of will. He simply has no resistance to drugs. When he takes one, he craves more. You're getting the best possible treatment in an attempt to put your cancer in remission. Ben should have the same chance."

When Julian didn't respond, I got tougher. "Ira said sometimes Ben stays away from home for days. That tells me your son knows how to survive on the streets in L.A.— which means drug connections, stealing, and, for some, prostitution."

Sarah winced, but Julian's somber expression told me I might finally be getting through to him. I continued, "If we were to put him in a treatment center here, he could run back to the streets. I'd like you to consider admitting him into a treatment center out of state. I'll give you the names of several to investigate."

Sarah said, "Good."

I was acutely aware that Julian still hadn't agreed to the intervention.

But I persevered as if he had. "Because Ben has difficulty facing problems, we're going to need lots of firepower at the intervention. I'd like people who have a positive influence on Ben and whom he'd be too embarrassed to run away from."

Sarah named several: her own parents; a former coach, the high school counselor, two others.

She finished with, "But more than anyone, you, Julian."

I nodded, looking directly at him. "You could contribute so much to the intervention—your thoughtfulness and love. Frankly, if we do this, I'm going to need all you can give me."

Julian nodded and said softly, "All right."

I felt my whole body relax, as if I'd just finished a long run.

I asked Sarah to contact the people she had named and set up a preparation session for tomorrow evening. I said I would plan the intervention for Thursday morning, the day after tomorrow, knowing if we didn't act quickly, Julian could intellectualize his way right out of it.

After they left, I made a note to ask Ben's counselor if we could hold Ben's intervention in a counseling room at the high school during his first-period class. That was one place where he consistently showed up, if only to make a drug buy.

Both Ira and Sarah had told me Ben's counselor, Phyllis Avery, was an extremely dedicated young woman, a former history teacher who had gone back to college for a counseling degree after her younger sister died from a cocaine overdose. Unresolved feelings over her sister's death made her zealously determined to save her addicted students. I've seen that kind of compensation many times. She hadn't faced her sister's addiction while the girl was still alive, and the sense of guilt over steps not taken would linger.

I wish I could make people understand until someone acts against addiction, the bad days just get worse, and many times people die.

Later that afternoon, Sarah called, still sounding strong and determined. She said she and Julian had decided on a treatment center in Oregon for Ben and she'd made plane reservations for Julian and Ben and me on a flight to Portland the day after tomorrow.

Then she went on to say the preparation meeting Wednesday night was going to be held at Ben's vice-principal's house, and gave me the address.

She'd been successful in lining up everyone except Paul Mayhew, once Ben's close friend.

"Isn't it funny," she said, "how different memories come back at you? I remember sitting in the stands with Paul's mother watching one of their junior high baseball games. I opened a thermos of coffee I'd brought and this strong liquor smell came out. It had to have been in the thermos before I poured in the coffee.

"I made a joke out of it, said I guessed the boys had been experimenting.

"Paul's mother didn't think it was funny, and from that day on she started putting restrictions on their friendship. Only I didn't know it. Especially since whenever Ben wanted to go out in those days, he'd tell Julian and me he was going to be with Paul, knowing we approved of Paul. It wasn't until I ran into Paul one day and asked him why he never came to the house any more that I found out he'd scarcely seen Ben in months.

"I take it he said no to participating in the intervention?"

"Yes. But Ed, I wondered if you could talk to him."

I had to tell her I might not be able to change his mind.

I've learned I can't depend on teenage peers to help in interventions. Sometimes they're too involved with drugs themselves. Or they'll have such a misguided sense of in-group loyalty that they'll tell the addicted person an intervention is being planned.

When I called Paul Mayhew's home, his mother answered. She asked my name, and when I told her, volunteered she wasn't in favor of Paul's participating in an intervention.

I asked why.

She said Ben's drinking was a family problem and the Knights shouldn't expect outsiders to become involved.

At the beginning of my career, I expended a great deal of energy trying to persuade such people to change their minds. I rarely succeeded.

I told Mrs. Mayhew I was sorry she felt that way, and asked to speak to her son.

Sounding reluctant, she called him to the phone.

Paul came on the line indignantly opposed to the intervention, telling me it would wreck any chance Ben had of graduating. And to take him to another state was the equivalent of kidnapping. "Ben just isn't that much of a drinker!"

Sometimes I wish I had something tangible I could show people and say, "Here. See what it looks like? That's addiction." I can point out its physical manifestations—the cirrhotic livers, gout, bleeding ulcers, ascites from alcoholism; cocaine's erosion of nasal membranes, damage to heart and liver. The list is long for each substance of abuse. But people who don't want to face their family member's or their friend's or their own addiction will assign other causes to those maladies—stress or unhappiness or poor eating habits. An addicted person may even go to a physician for help, not tell the physician how much drugs or alcohol he or she is consuming, and get prescription drugs or special diets to alleviate the distress. But such relief won't last, because the addicted person is only treating the symptom.

"How long has it been," I asked Paul, "since you spent any time with Ben?"

A moment of silence. "Two, three years. Not since junior high, I guess. We're not interested in the same things anymore. But I see him around to say hi to, and I think he's basically okay. My mother said—" He stopped.

"Go on."

"She said the reason Ben drinks is that too much is expected of him. His sister is on a merit scholarship at Stanford. His brother is a top-ranking golfer. And he's—just Ben."

That was a typical reaction from someone who doesn't accept the disease nature of addiction. People don't try to explain the emotional circumstances underlying a person's getting leukemia or multiple sclerosis or cancer. When I ask them why they impose that kind of explanation on addiction, they say because it's something people do to themselves. No one goes out and buys a leukemia germ and swallows it.

Perhaps in the initial stage of addiction, a person might find relief in dedication to work, religion, or marriage and could cling to abstinence—just as in the initial stage of a life-threatening disease a person's immune system might overcome it. But when the body can't summon enough defenses to fight any longer, it surrenders to the disease. The same thing happens in addiction.

I said, "You knew Ben was suspended from school this year, didn't you?"

"Yeah. I heard it was because he mouthed off at some teacher."

"Paul, Ben was suspended because he was drunk on campus, had a pint in his pocket and marijuana in his locker."

"Oh. Well . . ."

I could almost see the shrug.

"Did you know Ben hasn't gotten better than a D in any subject for a year and a half?"

"Come on," Paul said. "Ben's one of the brightest guys I know."

"Not anymore. You heard he'd been arrested twice, didn't you, for drunkenness and disturbing the peace?"

"No."

"And that he had to have extensive dental surgery after his front teeth were knocked out? He was so drunk he never remembered the fight."

A beat of silence. "No."

"After that, he either jumped or fell out of a third-story window when he was stoned."

"God."

"Paul, is it possible you're keeping the Ben who used to be your friend inside your head and you don't really know the person he is now?"

I could hear the agitation in Paul's voice as he said, "Listen, from kindergarten through junior high, we did everything together. Then my mom said he was a bad influence and I had to try and learn not to miss him."

"He got sick, Paul."

"But I still can't be at the intervention. I'd probably say all the wrong things. I might even . . ." He didn't finish.

I understood Paul believed he might cry. I wished I could tell him that was okay.

I said, "I respect your decision and I don't want to push you into something you feel uncomfortable about. But I want you to understand why we're intervening."

"I do," he said. "I just can't be there."

Wednesday night, the storm that had been hovering for two days materialized as I left my house to drive to Ben's vice-principal's house. Heavy showers plopped raindrops on my windshield, and then the rain turned into the steady driving kind I knew could last for days.

The meeting was set for 7:30, but I always like to be early so I can acclimate myself to my surroundings. It was a little after 7:00 when I got there. The living room that Al, the vice-principal, led me into had comfortable-looking over-stuffed chairs and a leather couch. A fire crackled in a big stone fireplace. It was a cheerful room to come into out of the storm.

Al's wife and teenage daughter were just leaving to go to a movie. As he introduced us, his daughter stared at me ingenuously and said, "I wondered what you were going to be like."

I suspect the word "interventionist" sometimes conjures up TV macho-man images, like the hero of "The Equalizer," and I think I disappointed her.

A small blond woman was warming her hands in front of the fire, and she came forward to introduce herself, saying, "I'm Ben's counselor, Phyllis Avery." I could see evidence of the pain and guilt she'd gone through over the death of her sister in her face, but there was also strength and humor.

We talked about how to plan the intervention at the high school tomorrow. I said I wanted every possible precaution taken to protect Ben's privacy.

Phyllis agreed. "There's an audiovisual room we use for showing movies to small groups—I think it would do. It's at the far end of the library, away from student traffic."

I said it sounded fine.

Al volunteered to be the one to summon Ben out of his English class and bring him to us.

I said, "Be sure and soft-pedal it. Don't let it seem like there's any kind of emergency."

The other participants started arriving then: Jake Fowler, Ben's ex-baseball coach, and Julian and Sarah.

Sarah took me to one side to tell me in a hushed voice that Ben had taken her car that afternoon without permission. "Sometimes when he does that," she whispered worriedly, "he disappears for days."

Occasionally people who are going to be intervened with

sense something is about to happen. Either they abruptly stop using whatever they are addicted to and begin to behave in an exemplary fashion, or they step up their use of the substance. If that was what Ben was doing, I hoped whatever he was on would run out before tomorrow.

But I told Sarah not to worry, we were going ahead exactly as planned.

Her parents were the last to arrive.

Sarah's father was a retired army colonel, a wizened, peppery man in his early seventies who was defensive about his grandson's problems, and I quickly realized it was because he had once been an excessive drinker himself. "Damned if I don't think a tough session of boot camp would be the best thing for him," he said. "I remember a top sergeant or two who straightened out young men in worse shape than Ben is. So, Mr. Storti, you tell me why you don't think that would be appropriate for my grandson."

I said that since liquor and marijuana are freely available in the army, Ben would go right on using; that Ben had a disease. The discipline he needed to put that disease in remission would be cultivated and reinforced during treatment.

My acknowledging the need for discipline seemed to satisfy the colonel, and we went on with the preparation.

After asking each person to describe his or her relationship with Ben, I discussed ways they could verbalize their love and concern and at the same time express their conviction he needed treatment.

Studying their faces as they listened, I couldn't help thinking how generous these people were: Sarah and Julian, who were going through so much personal trauma but were reaching out to help; the grandparents, who didn't comprehend the drug culture, yet overriding their confusion was love for their grandson; vice-principal Al Haven, who talked about seeing teenagers swallowed up by addiction; Coach Jake Fowler, who'd been certain three years ago Ben was headed for the major leagues; Phyllis Avery, sublimating her personal grief by investing her energy in keeping the living alive.

I pictured Ben walking into the small room off the library tomorrow where these people would be waiting. What would he do?

When I woke up Thursday, the rain was coming down in sheets. I hoped the storm wouldn't get bad enough to delay flights out of Los Angeles. I believed Ben's intervention was going to be difficult, and could picture how hard it might be to keep him from bolting at the airport—especially if he'd been drinking a lot and smoking marijuana the day before.

Driving to the high school, I stopped at my church long enough to go inside and light a candle for Ben. That's something I always do before an intervention—in my own church if I'm home, in whatever church I can find if I'm away.

I arrived at the high school a little after 8:00. Phyllis Avery was there to meet me and lead the way to the audio visual room. When we got there, I asked that the chairs be arranged in a circle.

The participants started arriving at 8:30. I worked to relax them as I indicated where I wanted them to sit, leaving an empty chair for Ben between his father and Coach Fowler, directly across from me.

Ben's grandparents were the most nervous—especially the colonel, though he tried to cover it up with an assertive attitude. As diplomatically as I could, I told him I'd be relying on him for the strong support I knew he could give me, but there could be only one person in charge this morning.

He grumbled a little, but when his wife said, "Oh, Arthur, behave," he looked a little sheepish, and subsided.

At 8:50, Al Hagen went to get Ben.

The tension in the room immediately shot up.

Just after the first-period buzzer sounded, Al returned with Ben.

Though not as wan as he had been the day I saw him in the hospital, he nevertheless showed physical deterioration. His eyes were dull, and he had the expression I'd grown accustomed to in addicted teenagers: a blend of defiance and desperation.

He stopped and stood in the doorway. "What the hell is this!"

It was a tense moment, rife with the possibility he might run, and his attitude, tone of voice, and expression spun me into a flashback on a teenage girl I'd intervened with a few months before.

When I told that girl I wanted to talk about her drug use, she'd said, "Uh-uh, forget *that*," and headed out of the room. Her mother tried to block the door. The girl hit out; the mother slapped her back. But the teenager got out the door and ran down the street and disappeared. Within seconds, a carefully planned intervention had shattered. And even though she did go into treatment five days later as a direct result of her emotional response to the fact that an intervention had been planned, after she bolted that morning the people who had gathered in her home had to deal with her having run away.

It can happen, especially with teenagers. I knew it could happen here as I said, "Ben, my name is Ed Storti. Come on in and sit down in the chair next to your dad."

Ben was confused, and intimidated enough by the roomful of people to do what I said, but demanded, "What's this about?"

I said, "We're here because we have something important to tell you. Before we begin, I want to say I hope you know how lucky you are to have these people who love and respect you."

He just repeated, "What's it all about?"

"It's about the problems you're having with alcohol and marijuana."

He stood up. "I'm not going to listen to this."

"Please stay sitting right where you are," I told him. "The people in this room have jobs to go to, work to do, other places they're supposed to be. But they've put their own schedules aside to come here and talk, and I want you to do them the courtesy of listening."

Julian had reached out while I was speaking to gently touch Ben's knee. I don't know if that's what did it or not, but the boy sat down again.

I said, "Ben, I want you to know something. I have the same disease you do—addiction."

The look he gave me—a superior smile—let me know he wasn't interested in a thing I was saying. While working as a probation officer, I'd reached a saturation point with adolescent smart-ass looks and figured out a way to handle them. I don't let my anger show. If I'm not getting the response I want, I pretend I am. Sometimes it convinces them, sometimes me, or even both of us.

So I ignored his spare-me-your-lecture expression and, knowing I was going to have to be firm with this kid, not let him steamroll the people in this room or me, I talked about addiction, described things I knew he was going through based on what people had told me the night before.

Then I said, "I've worked in this field eleven years. I know the disease. You've got it. And you're going to hear from these people how every phase of your life—family, school, athletics, social—is being destroyed by it."

I'd told my participants during the preparation that when I called on them, there couldn't be any hesitation, because Ben would fill the silence with denials or else he'd run.

When I nodded at Al Hagen, he started speaking as quickly and forcefully as I'd hoped, saying, "Ben, at the beginning of your freshman year, I could tell you were having problems, and I've watched those problems increase.

We follow a rigid disciplinary process in dealing with drug addiction on this campus. While it's my job to carry that out, I never forget that behind the problem is a person. So I'm glad for this chance to tell you I care, that I want you to go into treatment and get well, that I'll do anything within my power to help."

Ben's expression remained the same—insolent, indifferent.

But I'd expected that. I said, "Aren't you sick of trying to convince people you're okay when you feel terrible?"

"I'm fine!" he insisted.

I nodded quickly at Phyllis Avery.

"I have your file right here." She held it up. "So far this semester, you have three F's, two D's; you've put in forty-five hours of detention."

Phyllis was more impersonal than I'd expected or wanted her to be as she went on citing the statistics corroborating Ben's failures. But her expression told me how hard she was trying to stay away from the ghost of her sister and remain objective.

She said, "If you agree to go into a treatment center, I'll arrange for your readmittance to school when you come out and I will work with you as hard as I can to make it possible for you to graduate."

Ben shouted, "I don't care if I graduate, I'm not going into any damn hospital, so get off my back!"

Phyllis blinked away sudden tears.

At that, Ben's grandfather couldn't hold back any longer. He said, "Dammit, boy, take a look at yourself! Do you want to spend the rest of your life in the terrible shape you're in now?"

"How I spend my life is my business," Ben snapped, but I could tell he was shaken a little.

I said, "It isn't just your business. Seven people have come here because what you're doing is affecting *their* lives, too. Addiction is a selfish disease. You keep taking and using and deteriorating and you think people who care about you aren't affected by that?

"Laura," I said to Ben's grandmother, "what can you say about it?"

She shook her head. Between sobs she was trying to control, she said, "I can't talk. I'm sorry."

However much you coach people what to say, you never really know whether they'll be able to or not. Ben's grandmother couldn't. But her presence was powerful, and so were her tears.

I looked at Ben. "Does it mean anything to you, what's happening to your grandmother?"

Without giving him a chance to respond, I turned to Jake Fowler. "Coach?"

Jake pulled his chair forward and turned it at an angle until his knees were almost touching Ben's. "You were one of the hottest ballplayers I've ever seen. I'll never forget the day you showed up for a crucial game stoned and I had to tell you to turn in your uniform. What the hell happened? You loved baseball in the way truly gifted players do, and you wouldn't have turned your back on it if something hadn't fallen apart. What? Ben, you haven't let anybody help you find out. It's time you did."

The boy shook his head. "I don't want help."

"You don't have to want it," I said. "If you're going to survive, you must accept it."

And I went immediately to Ben's mother.

Sarah's voice was firm and determined as she said, "I still set a place for you at the table even though it's been weeks since you sat down with us. Each time I look at your chair, I picture you alone and drunk. Maybe dead. So you listen to me. I'm not going to put myself through that anymore, I mean it. Either you—"

"Don't give me orders! Shut up!" Ben cut her off.

"Benjamin!" The colonel stood up. I was glad he didn't have a weapon. He would have used it on Ben.

"Colonel," I said, "please sit down."

He glared at me until his wife tugged on his coat sleeve.

I knew Ben was trying to abort the intervention by attacking people, and I said, putting some steel in it, "Ben, please let people finish what they have to say. They are trying to help you save your life, and you're acting as if they have no right to do that. Can you tell me why you don't believe your life is worth saving?"

Something in Ben's expression flickered briefly, making me sure I'd reached him, if only for an instant.

At once I said, "Julian?"

Ben gave his father a quick sidelong glance. Then his head went down and he fastened his eyes on his sneakers.

Julian looked especially unwell. It was obvious he hadn't slept the night before. I could tell how difficult it was going to be for him to speak. But if he didn't, I believed the intervention was doomed.

At last he said in that soft Kentucky cadence, "Son, I'm fighting to live, and you're trying to die. What makes us so different?"

Ben's head stayed down. He didn't say a word.

His responses had been so quick until this moment, I knew something was happening inside him now. The time seemed right to move toward closing. I went on, "Ben, you've heard everyone say you need help. You know it yourself. Arrangements have been made for you at an excellent treatment center in Oregon. Your parents chose it because they want you to make a fresh start."

His head jerked up, and his expression, which had softened when Julian spoke, went hard again. "Oregon!" he said. "Screw that!"

I'd expected this, so I said, "Okay, Ben, I hear you. But just let me tell you a little about the good things that have been planned." I talked about the group and family counseling sessions, the fact that all the Knights would soon be spending a week with him. Even his sister was flying in from college.

Then I started around my circle again.

They all spoke this time, including Ben's grandmother.

After studying him as they spoke, I observed, "One of your major problems is, you're bored with life. It's in your face and attitude. And that's incredible, with your mind and talent."

Suddenly Julian turned so his whole body was facing Ben, his level gray eyes holding his son's. "How can I make you understand? With all our differences, you're like me. No choices left. You must accept whatever treatment will help you."

Ben's eyes filled with tears, and he brushed them away angrily. "Are you going to get better?"

Julian asked, "Are you?"

"Oh, Jesus."

I moved in, talking about the people on the staff at the treatment center, the gym, the basketball court, cottages, snow, forests, clean air. I probably sounded as if I worked for the Oregon Tourist Board, but as I talked, I sensed a niche opening in Ben's resistance.

The final issue for him was "What will my friends think?"

Compared to what we'd just come through, that was easy.

I said, "Your best friends are right here, so what friends do you mean? The dopers, drinkers, and dropouts? It's bad for them because they don't have the love and support you do. But you've got a chance. Look—your dad has the plane tickets in his pocket."

That startled him.

He said to Julian, "You don't."

His father drew the folder from his breast pocket.

Ben looked at it. He didn't say anything.

It was going to be a slow drive to the airport in the rain. I said to Julian, "We'd better leave soon."

Julian stood up and said, "Come on, son, it's time to go." After a moment's hesitation, Ben stood up, too.

Minutes later, I was driving around to the side door where they were all waiting, and Ben and Julian got in the car.

The others left the shelter of the doorway to come out and stand watching us drive away. I kept glancing in the rearview mirror until I turned the corner. The time we'd spent together had formed a bond. It's always hard to let go of that.

During the forty-minute drive to the airport, Ben murmured once, "I don't believe I'm doing this."

Julian put his arm across his son's shoulders, and Ben didn't say anything more.

At the airport, I could tell from the slump of his shoulders and his slow reactions that Ben was under the residual influence of THC. I wasn't surprised when he slept most of the way on the plane as well as on the drive to the treatment center in Salem.

When we arrived, two counselors in ski parkas came out to greet us. New-fallen snow covered the ground, but the storm that had brought it had passed. I hoped the Knights' storm had passed, too.

A few months after Ben's intervention, the Knights told me of their deep involvement in the family-counseling week in Salem. Sarah said, "We discovered how we had helped Ben remain addicted, and we talked about relapse symptoms for him, and for the family. We were able to tell Ben in a very personal way how we'd been hurt. And we also had a chance to tell him what we loved about him when he was straight. It was healing to get it all said."

A year after Ben left the treatment center, he suffered a relapse and started drinking excessively and using marijuana again.

Sarah and Julian (whose cancer had gone into remission) told Ben they would always be there to offer constructive help when he was ready to accept it. But through the insights they gained from intervening, participation in intensive family counseling, and their subsequent involvement in a parent self-help group, they would no longer accept, protect, or nurture his addiction.

As difficult as it often is for parents to intervene with their addicted children, their ability to do so is reinforced by the caretaking role they are expected to play in their children's lives.

It's a more complex and difficult situation when those roles are reversed and adult children who still have operant memories of their parents as all-knowing and omnipotent decide they must intervene with a parent's addiction. That kind of intervention is more likely to evoke intrafamily strife than any other. And it's especially hard when a child has to oppose one parent, in order to try to help another.

Sol and Suzanne

It was a warm, springlike week in early February when Suzanne Silberman called to discuss having me intervene with her father, Sol.

Suzanne was an intense, dark-haired young woman in her late twenties. Four years earlier, she had moved away from her family in the East—parents, brother, aunt—to live in Los Angeles.

She described her father as a work-driven jeweler who had been alcoholic as far back as she could remember. As a child, she'd accepted his drinking, and had no awareness of the inroads the disease was making on his health. But after she moved and saw her father only two or three times a year, she became aware of his deterioration.

Before calling me, she'd contacted her relatives to determine whether they would be willing to participate in an intervention. Her brother and aunt were emphatically in favor of it. Her mother was not.

"But that's because she's always added so much to my father's disease," Suzanne said, giving the nervous little laugh I noticed accompanied her discussion of sensitive issues. "She runs his drinking like other women run their households."

I said, "I understand."

It was another instance of a spouse having collaborated with the disease of addiction so intensely the thought of that collaboration ending was actually frightening. In all such cases, I try to win spouses over. If I can't, I'm often reluctant to intervene and will recommend a self-help group or counseling for that spouse.

Suzanne listened as I explained this, said she knew her mother wouldn't be easy to persuade, but asked me to call her and try.

I said I would.

My phone conversation with Mrs. Silberman affirmed she was the most intense kind of collaborator. She said Sol was too old to change and stated a man with his background had the right to do anything he wanted, and that included drinking.

I learned Sol's family had had to flee Nazi Germany in 1938. Sol had been twelve when he escaped with his parents and sister through Poland into France, where he remained in a work camp for three years. The family emigrated to the United States in 1941, but Sol's parents were ill and impoverished then, and Sol had supported them and his sister from the day of their arrival in America.

Because of Mrs. Silberman's attitude, I had grave doubts about intervening with Sol. I told Suzanne that.

Her response was to beg me to do the intervention despite her mother.

It was an interventionist's Catch-22 I'd been through several times. I don't have a hard-and-fast rule about accepting or rejecting family interventions if a crucial family member refuses to participate. Each such situation has its own dynamics, and I try to weigh the probable outcome as best I can. I don't always make the right decision. A few months before Suzanne called me, I'd told a son who wanted me to intervene with his alcoholic mother despite his father's vehement opposition, no, I couldn't do it. Six months later, the woman died. Perhaps the intervention wouldn't have worked—but perhaps it would have.

So even knowing Sol's intervention might be sabotaged by his wife, I found it difficult to refuse Suzanne's request.

At her urging, I had a few more conversations with Mrs. Silberman, trying to convince her the intervention would bring about positive results in Sol's life and her own. Suzanne and her brother, Nathan, also talked to her, and she finally gave her consent. Reluctantly. I hoped when we met face to face, I could completely win her over.

Suzanne arranged to have her father admitted to a treatment center close to her home in Los Angeles. Then she made reservations for us to fly to New York.

I planned to hold the preparation session at Suzanne's brother's apartment on a Friday evening, the intervention the next morning, and Suzanne and Sol and I would fly back to California in the afternoon.

It was my first long flight with a family member, and it taught me that I needed to prepare for such journeys, just as I did for interventions. I'd planned to let my "performance adrenaline" build during the flight, and inside my head, go over things I intended to say. But Suzanne was anxious, and therefore talkative. She voiced for the first time her fear that her father might be immovable, and she needed a lot of reassuring that even if her mother withdrew her support, the intervention could still succeed.

That trip happened to be my first to the East Coast. When we'd left Los Angeles, the temperature had been in the mid-seventies. I had on thin socks, and had brought only a fold-up-in-a-pocket raincoat. When we stepped off the plane, the wind chill made me wonder if we'd landed in the Yukon. But after we were in a taxi in bumper-to-bumper traffic on a clogged expressway, I felt more at home.

Suzanne's relatives were all waiting when we got to Nathan's.

Nathan, face to face, was a muscular, verbally aggressive

young man. Within moments of our being introduced, he told me he'd received an award for outstanding oratory in law school and I could count on him to really speak up during the intervention.

Aunt Miriam was a plump, kind-faced woman in her early sixties. She expressed deep fondness for her brother, telling me with tears in her eyes, "Sol saved us during the war, you know. If I can help him now, I will be repaying only a little of what I owe him."

Because of her emotion and also because it reflected on things Mrs. Silberman had said, I should have asked more about that. A lot more. If I had, things might have gone differently.

Mrs. Silberman was fluttery, vague, and unstable. Since our last phone conversation, she had again formed resistance to the idea of intervening.

So I concentrated on preparing the others.

Wary of Nathan's overassertiveness, I worked especially hard to clarify the "loving son" role I wanted him to project. But he kept saying, "Listen, my dad can be tough. If you get tired and want me to take over for a while, you just give me the high sign."

Aunt Miriam was warm and intuitive, and grasped quickly what I wanted from her.

Suzanne's anxious desire for everything to go smoothly made her edgy and prone to that nervous laughter. Still, I was confident she'd say the right things.

Finally, I tried for a minimal commitment from Mrs. Silberman, saying, "If I call on you and ask you to tell your husband one thing, that you want him to get help, can you do that?"

Her "Yes" was almost whispered.

At the end of the preparation, I had to acknowledge I didn't have anyone with real power over Sol. Nathan was too young and overconfident. Aunt Miriam was nurturing but not forceful. Suzanne gave me no sense of strength. She'd thought it was there, yet she'd been fragmenting ever since we'd left California. That left me. I'd been my own power person in other interventions where the group was weak. But after hours in a plane with Suzanne, a long taxi ride, dealing with the family, and now facing a night in a strange hotel room, I'd have to dig deep for the energy.

It was past midnight by the time Nathan drove me to my hotel, and a little before 7:00 when he and Suzanne picked me up the next morning. Nathan, as enthusiastic a driver as he was a speaker, zoomed in and out of the moderate Saturday-morning traffic to reach the Silbermans' small, well-kept home in Brooklyn.

I expected Mrs. Silberman to open the door, but Sol did.

Suzanne had told me that even when her father was sober, he had a tendency to be unkempt, and when he was drinking he became even more so. That morning, he hadn't shaved, his shirttail was out in back, and he had on baggy wool pants covered with cat hair. He was small and thin and round-shouldered and looked as if a short gust of wind could blow him away. And yet, the night before, all the Silbermans had said how strong he was. Seeing his physical deterioration, I concluded that the strength his family attributed to him was simply the mythical strength frequently given to the ill. A grave mistake on my part.

Seeing Suzanne, his face lit up. "Suzu, I didn't know you were coming for a visit." Then he noticed Nathan, Miriam, and me, and his smile broadened. "So," he said, holding out his hand to me, "are you the boyfriend?"

I explained I had come to discuss a sensitive issue and suggested we go inside and sit and talk. The welcome in his eyes was replaced by suspicion, but he courteously led the way into the living room, where Mrs. Silberman was seated stiffly on the edge of a chair. After everyone was seated, I told Sol this meeting had been planned out of the love his family had for him and their concern about his diminishing health because of drinking. Then I went on to discuss alcoholism in depth.

I'd worked hard at getting myself "up"; my adrenaline was high, and I knew I was presenting well.

When I called on Suzanne, Nathan, and Aunt Miriam for support, all spoke effectively, saying what we'd prepared even more movingly than I had hoped.

I was pleased at how smoothly things were going until I got to Mrs. Silberman and asked whether she believed Sol should get help. She didn't look at any of us, just murmured so we almost couldn't hear her, "Sol must do whatever he believes is right."

Suzanne flashed her mother a knife-edged look, and I could tell she was about to attack. Family discord can destroy an intervention in seconds, so I put my hand on Suzanne's and quickly rephrased Mrs. Silberman's words. "In her own way, Sol, your wife wants you to get better, just as we all do."

Suzanne subsided, and I thought we were back on course.

Actually, we never had been, because contrary to my first impression, Sol was formidable. At that stage of my career, I hadn't encountered intellectually aggressive tactics like his—though I have several times since.

Sol didn't argue. He teased my sentences apart, extricated words, analyzed the concepts behind those words, which led him into discussions far afield—all red herrings to draw focus away from his drinking. If I grew impatient he would give the impression he was on the verge of agreeing to go for treatment. Then, as soon as I relaxed, he'd retrench, saying "Wait, I want to think some more."

Starting out at Sol's house that morning with our return flight not due to depart until 6:00 P.M., I'd been willing, initially, to give him all the time he needed to think.

By noon I was less willing.

At 3:00 P.M., I'd heard him say "You may be right, I'm just not sure" too many times.

I was exhausted. So were Suzanne and Miriam. But Sol

didn't look any different than he had when he'd opened the door at 9:00 A.M.

Nathan said, "Listen, let me talk to him for a while."

If I'd thought it would have done a speck of good, I would have.

I said, "Sol, I'm calling in the cards. I've given you all I have to give. What are you going to do?"

He said, "I need a little more time."

"We're out of time. I want an answer."

He knew I meant it.

"Well, Ed, I don't think I'm going to California with you today. Maybe in a few weeks I'll fly out and have a look."

Beaten into the ground, I nevertheless tried to sound positive. "If you really mean it, Sol, that's wonderful."

We shook hands, and with that he offered to drive Suzanne and me to the airport.

She was furious. "Nathan will!" But Nathan had to take his aunt home—in the opposite direction from the airport, so if we were going to make our flight, our only other option was to call a cab. Sol wouldn't hear of it.

"He thinks he's won," Suzanne muttered as we were walking out to the car.

He had. No contest. *This* round. I whispered, "His disease won the skirmish, Suzanne. To me, the only intervention that totally fails is the one not attempted. Who knows? Maybe he heard us. I think he did."

"Sure."

I took her arm. "You can get past this. If you let yourself be pulled back into agonizing over his disease, it means there's an attraction in you to his behavior just as he is attracted to holding on to his disease. You've got to let go now."

During the drive to the airport, the only conversation was between Sol and me, though I could tell by his frequent glances in the rearview mirror that he wanted to make up with his daughter.

When we were getting out of the car, she said to him, "I don't know when or if I'll see you again. I've got to find some peace."

Sol leaned out the window and tried to take her hand. She wouldn't let him.

He smiled. "Suzu, I don't blame you for what happened today. You thought you were doing the right thing."

"I was," she said, and picking up her suitcase, she walked away.

He sat staring after her a few moments, then pulled away from the curb, and his car soon disappeared in the flow of traffic.

On the flight home, I worked hard to help Suzanne release herself from her involvement with her father's addiction, and I kept in close touch with her in the following weeks to be certain she was all right. I encouraged her to join a support group and seek therapy and was relieved, for her sake, when she did.

Sol lingered in my mind for a long time.

One evening, I was discussing his case over dinner with some colleagues. A counselor I knew only slightly, a man in his early sixties with a soft European accent, said, "Ed, I don't think anyone who came out of a pogrom or a work camp would admit himself for treatment. Any outside control takes on terrible meaning for people like Sol. That's what you were dealing with."

Listening, I could almost see Sol's face: the wispy gray hair and sad eyes, in contrast to the implacable jaw.

Suzanne called me six months after my intervention with her father and reported that she and Sol had exchanged several emotional letters. As a result, he had enrolled in an outpatient program in New York City, was attending self-help groups, and seemed to be on the road to recovery.

"So you were right," Suzanne said. "He did hear us after all."

I grinned and thought, "God bless the wily old scoundrel." He had taught me more than he would ever know.

———————

The lives of many adult children in our society are deeply affected by an elderly parent's addiction. Suzanne, after moving thousands of miles away from her family, attained sufficient objectivity about her father's addiction to become determined to act against it.

But not all children can be objective.

Ted, Dorothy . . . and Cass

Ted Bixby, a bachelor in his early thirties, was a consulting engineer who traveled all over the world. He sat across from me in my office late one November afternoon, his dark brown eyes anxious as he told me why he'd asked for an appointment.

During a recent trip east, he'd stopped in Boston to visit his mother at her retirement residence. As he was leaving, a resident of the home, a man named Myron Walton, took him aside and said he'd been chosen as kind of a delegate by the other people in the home to speak to Ted about Cass's drinking.

Myron told Ted there were enough empty gin bottles under Cass's bed to stock a small distillery. He said she no longer had a good relationship with anyone except the delivery boy from the liquor store and was usually "too much in her cups" even to want to participate in the biweekly outings the other people in the home took such pleasure from. Worst of all, she smoked heavily while she was drinking and frequently dozed off with a burning cigarette in her hand; she had set fire to her chair twice. On the occasions she managed to stay on her feet while she was drinking, she stumbled and bumped into things. So far she'd only gotten scrapes and bruises, but Myron was afraid one day soon she might fall and seriously injure herself.

Ted told me his sister, Dorothy, lived in Boston and visited their mother two or three times a week. When he'd spoken about Cass's excessive drinking, Dorothy told him she was aware their mother drank "a little too much." She was rationing Cass's consumption of alcohol by taking her only a quart of gin per week.

Ted mentioned the liquor store's deliveries and Dorothy said that was just retirement-home gossip and Myron Walton was exaggerating. Their mother might order an extra bottle for a holiday or special occasion, but that was it.

Ted then told his sister it sounded to him like Cass shouldn't be drinking at all, and Dorothy responded defensively, stating that since he was so seldom on the scene he had no business drawing conclusions. Having a highball or two in the evening had become their mother's greatest, perhaps only, pleasure in life.

It was after that conversation with Dorothy that Ted decided to contact me.

His eyes held mine steadily as he asked whether I thought an intervention with his eighty-one-year-old mother could be successful or whether it was even appropriate.

I said, "I do understand your uncertainty. When people learn I'm going to intervene on someone who is seventy-five years or more old, many say the same thing—essentially, 'Why take it away if it gives pleasure?' But that's doing the elderly a disservice. Motivating someone to enter a treatment center has nothing whatever to do with age. What's involved is quality of life. Anytime someone's dignity is being threatened by excessive use of a substance, that needs to be examined and the question 'Does it have to be this way?' has to be asked.

"It seems clear Cass's mental and physical condition is deteriorating. And beyond the damage alcohol is doing to her directly, her drinking puts her at grave risk of injury. I think we should intervene."

Looking relieved, Ted agreed. He said perhaps his sister's

attitude reflected the difficult life she had led, and it was probably time he assumed more responsibility for the care of their mother. He knew of an excellent treatment center in West Los Angeles, close to the townhouse where he lived. Since he had to be on the East Coast the week after Christmas, would I fly to Boston then, talk to Dorothy, and intervene with Cass?

I said I would.

Ted and I spoke on the phone several times before Christmas. I asked him to have Myron let the residents in the convalescent home know that I'd prepare them the morning of the intervention, and to make sure none of them told Cass about it. Each conversation we had, I sensed Ted becoming increasingly anxious at the prospect of intervening. Finally I asked what was wrong.

He said, "I think you should know you're going to have a difficult time convincing Dorothy. When I told her what I was planning, she was furious. I thought she'd cool off, but she hasn't. Just the opposite."

Children who have accepted the responsibility of caring for an elderly parent often become defensive, even enraged, when someone—even a sibling—tries to interfere. They have structured their existences around their obligations, and anything that alters that structure changes their lives. They don't like it.

I asked Ted if he wanted to call off the intervention.

After a long pause, he said, "No."

I said, "Good." By then a picture of Cass as this little old woman just rocking and drinking her life away had begun to form in my mind. There had to be more.

I told him, "I believe I can convince Dorothy we're doing the right thing."

He said nervously, "You'd better."

Winter is always a chancy time for travel. On December 30, my plane left Los Angeles on time, and it was a fairly smooth flight east. But as we were making our landing approach into Boston, the wing flaps suddenly went up and we ascended at full power back into the clouds.

I'd experienced aborted landings before, and I waited calmly for the customary soothing announcement from the captain. But the intercom was silent. Soon the passengers stopped chatting among themselves while the stewardesses sat grim-faced in their jump seats behind the captain's compartment. I'd never experienced such silence inside an airplane. I thought, "This is it. We're going down."

Someone nearby lit a cigarette. I'd stopped smoking twelve years ago when I stopped drinking. But now, "last chance" thoughts were going through my mind. I wished I had a cigarette.

As I sat contemplating a quick death, the captain's voice came over the intercom. He told us a warning light had flashed briefly on the instrument panel. He was now confident everything was normal, but crash trucks had been summoned to stand by for our landing and we shouldn't be alarmed when we saw them waiting on the ground.

My heightened fear receptors registered only two words: "crash trucks." When I saw their red lights flashing below, I knew I wasn't going to leave the plane in one piece.

Of course I did. The landing was smooth, uneventful. And we humans forget our pain so easily. By the time I met Ted in the terminal, I was relaxed and cheerful.

He wasn't. The aborted landing had delayed my arrival by forty minutes, and he was anxious about the time. I'd hoped to be able to check into my hotel before going to Dorothy's, but Ted asked if I'd mind going straight there. He looked so dour, I asked, "What's up?"

He shook his head. "To be honest, Ed, I feel like I've set you up. I probably should have called the whole thing off. You're not going to be able to persuade my sister to consent to the intervention."

I said confidently, "Well, since I'm here, I might as well try."

The confidence was part show, part real. Ted seemed so apprehensive, the coward in me didn't want to tangle with Dorothy. But the rest of me was curious.

Slushy snow covered the ground, and a cold sleety rain was falling as we drove into Boston. Ted pulled up in front of a tall, narrow house with darkly draped windows. We walked up a short flight of steps, and Ted unlocked a door he had to push hard on to open. Then he led me down a long hallway into a gloomy kitchen.

Dorothy was doing dishes at the sink. She was a tall, heavyset woman with gray hair. As we entered, she turned and said almost accusingly, "I suppose you're Mr. Storti?"

"That's right." I smiled. "I'm happy to meet you."

She said, "You're late."

Near one wall, there was an eating counter with wooden stools in front of it. Dorothy pointed to the one she wanted me to sit on. "Just so we're clear, Mr. Storti, I don't intend to have a thing to do with this intervention business. I think it's very wrong. But since you've come all this way, Ted says I must listen to you."

On the way in from the airport, I'd asked him to tell me a little about Dorothy. He'd said she was a surgical nurse, had been married briefly and unhappily to an alcoholic. He'd thought she'd needed help resolving the trauma of her divorce, but she'd never gotten any, asserting she was fully capable of handling her own problems. After the divorce, she'd lived with and cared for their mother up until the time Cass had decided to move into the retirement home.

Looking at Dorothy, I could see how darkness had seeped into all the corners of her life. I sensed whoever "Dorothy" might once have been was now buried in years of pain and martyrdom. She was a classic example of the adult child of an alcoholic.

She went on, "I realize you and Ted will do whatever it is you feel you have to. But remember, when you leave, I'm the one who'll have to pick up the pieces. Like always."

I glanced at Ted. He looked subdued, defeated. In California, even as his confidence had started to wane, he'd maintained we would go ahead and do the intervention with or without his sister. No wonder he'd moved as far west as he could, I thought. Here in this house where he'd grown up with an alcoholic mother and a domineering sister, all his emotions were cued. He was watching Dorothy's face, gauging her expression, and I could tell his response to anything I said would be contingent on hers.

I said, "Dorothy, you agree, don't you, your mother has a drinking problem?"

"Of course," she said. "Any fool can see that. But taking her out to Hollywood and putting her in some hospital among drunken strangers isn't the answer. Here at least she has me to look after her."

Her words made it clear that playing caretaker was vital to her existence, a role she didn't want taken away.

I had to be careful, because Dorothy was stirring up the desire in me to go punch for punch in the ring with her. I'd been prone to do that when I first entered counseling and had quickly learned how destructive it could be. People ended up saying, "The hell with you, Storti." So I had to diffuse my antagonistic response quickly, because I realized the real intervention was taking place right here in Dorothy's kitchen. If I could persuade her, the "controller" in Cass's life, to tell her mother to go into treatment, I was 99 percent certain Cass would go.

I said, "Dorothy, please don't see me as your enemy. I'm here to help you as well as your mother. I don't think you should have to visit that retirement home every week, watching your mother slide farther downhill each time you see her. What kind of life is that for you?"

"I don't complain," she snapped, and turned to her brother. "When have you ever heard me complain?"

"Maybe you should complain," I said. "You have good

years ahead of you. So does your mom. Her disease doesn't have to be a prison cell for either of you."

Dorothy blinked at me. Her territory was the martyr's cell. She didn't know what to do with the thought of freedom. I suspected she even felt threatened by it.

I went on, "Picture how much easier your life would be if you knew your mother was getting help with her drinking problem. With your nursing background, you know taking her a quart of liquor a week isn't what you should be doing."

"I'm weaning her!" she replied angrily.

I said, "I'm convinced you think you're doing the right thing. But alcoholics have a way of getting as much liquor as they need. I admit I don't know what shape your mother is in, how far she's deteriorated. But whatever shape she's in, continuing to drink will only make her worse. We can extend the good time she has left by getting her into treatment."

Dorothy sighed, turned her back on me, and wrung out her dishrag.

I pressed on, "I once had an aunt in a nursing home. She had acute diabetes. When my father died, I was named her guardian, so I visited her every week. Coming out of that place I'd be so depressed, I'd be thinking, 'Is this all there is?'

"I believe you're doing that too, Dorothy, and you need brighter things to think about. Nobody could help my aunt. But there's help for Cass. She can get better. You'd be surprised at how much."

She shook her head, but the set of her shoulders wasn't quite as stiff as it had been.

Knowing I might be taking a chance now, but believing she needed to hear this from someone, I said, "Dorothy, once we get your mom into treatment, I'd like you to think about getting some help, too. Because with Cass in treatment, when she gets better, you might be tempted to replace her with someone else who wants you to be their support in life."

She sniffed. "That's California poppycock."

"Call it what you like. I just want you to know, you don't ever need to do that again."

I went on to relate some of the sad stories I knew about alcoholism's invasion of the lives of the elderly. I talked pretty much without interruption for over an hour. I explained the reason for taking Cass to California was to give her, Dorothy, time to stabilize and to allow Ted to become involved in Cass's treatment. I said I knew there were excellent therapy groups Dorothy could become involved with in Boston, and perhaps after some time had passed, she would feel like visiting Cass in California.

Dorothy finally capitulated the only way a "Dorothy" could. She said with a long-suffering sigh, "You've just worn me down. I'll have to go along with whatever you say. It doesn't really matter what *I* want."

I was so tired myself I was tempted to let that pass. But I couldn't. Allowing a person to participate in an intervention as a martyr entices him or her to turn on you.

I said, "Dorothy, I'd like you to participate in the intervention tomorrow. I think your being there could influence Cass a great deal, so I'm going to leave it up to you whether you participate or not. But if you do, when I ask you, in front of your mom, if you want her to get help, I need you to say, 'Yes, Mom, you must.' Can you do that?"

She gave a little derisive sniff, then a shrug, and finally a nod.

"Wonderful," I said warmly, standing up to leave. "Get a good night's sleep. I'll see you in the morning."

A Ted much more like the one I'd known in California drove me to my hotel. He was obviously heartened by my having won Dorothy over. And yet he also seemed a little distracted. After we'd been in the car about twenty minutes, he said, "Ed, I hate to throw this at you after what you've just been through with my sister, but I have to fly to London the day after tomorrow on urgent business. If the intervention is successful, would it be possible for you to fly back to

California alone with Cass and take her to the treatment center?"

The only predictable thing about an interventionist's life is that it's never predictable. I knew such a journey would be wearing. And yet, thinking how fine it would be if Cass could start the new year in treatment, I said, "Of course, and I'll treat her as if she were my own maiden aunt."

Later that night alone in my hotel room, I realized I'd never even seen Cass, had no idea how deteriorated she was or what it would be like to travel three thousand miles with her.

When Ted picked me up in front of the hotel the next morning, it was snowing. Boston looked beautiful. Lots of times I wish I could relax and enjoy the scenery in some of the places I visit, yet whatever case I'm working on has to be paramount in my mind.

Dorothy was sitting in the front passenger seat. As I got in the back, she responded to my good morning with a nod I would have missed seeing if I'd blinked.

The drive to the retirement home took only about twenty minutes. It was a dark red brick building with tiny windows.

When we entered the lobby, a tall thin old man with a straight back and a bald head came forward. He shook my hand, introducing himself as "Cass's friend Myron." He said there were half a dozen more of Cass's friends gathered in the lounge ready, willing, and able to help out.

So I went in and talked to them for a little while. They were such a willing group, I scarcely needed to prepare them. They listened earnestly to everything, and a few even took notes. I said, "What I need from you I can already see in your eyes. If she denies the drinking, tell her in a caring way you know she's drinking too much. If she's upset about going on the plane, encourage her. But mostly, just be there for her. With friends like you, I don't think we're going to lose her."

The day nurse came into the lounge to tell me Cass hadn't gotten up for breakfast, and that it looked like it was going to be one of her stay-in-bed-until-noon days.

I said that was fine, we would hold the intervention in Cass's room. I asked the nurse to lead the way.

Cass's room wasn't very big, maybe ten by twelve feet. It held her bed, a bureau, a chair, and a three-year-old calendar on the wall turned to the month of April. It had the dreary "convalescent odor" I'd encountered in other rooms where elderly people were giving up on life.

I asked Dorothy and Ted to stand on one side of the bed, Myron and his friends on the other. I stood at the foot.

Cass looked at all of us out of faded blue eyes. She was wasted-looking, pallid, her hair thin and gray, fingers brown with nicotine. The ruffle on the collar of her once-pink nightgown was spotted with food stains.

She said, "Goodness, is it my birthday?"

I said, "No, Cass. Ted and Dorothy and your friends and I have met and talked. People here tell me you've given pleasurable moments to all of them. Now they want to give you something—their care and concern. We all want you to get help for your drinking problem."

She started to cry. She knew. Wherever she'd gone in her alcoholic haze, it wasn't so far away that she didn't know she needed help.

I talked to her about alcoholism and how we wanted her to live a better life than she was presently living. I also described the arrangements Ted had made for her at a treatment center in southern California.

Myron spoke up then to tell her the last weather report he'd heard, the temperature in Los Angeles was seventy-two degrees, and he wished she'd hurry on out there and get better so she could invite him to come and visit. He said, "Cass, you used to be such fun. For a while, I was sweet on you. I could be again."

Cass's eyes took in all the faces: her friends', Myron's,

Ted's, Dorothy's. They lingered on Dorothy, and she asked meekly, "Dottie, is it all right?"

Addicted people often need someone else to make the decision for them—as Ben Knight had needed his dad.

Worry began to form in my mind as Cass's question hung unanswered. Dorothy's shoulders looked as if they were made of stone again.

I said, "Dorothy, what would you like your mother to do?"

She gave me a frown that would have cut paper. But that was all right, because the words that came out of her mouth were: "Yes, Mom, you go out to California and get some help."

Cass's eyes swung to me then. Her voice was anxious as she asked, "Who's going with me?"

"I am," I told her, smiling. "I'm going to fly with you to Los Angeles this afternoon and take care of you every mile of the way."

The day nurse, who'd been hovering in the hallway, entered the room, offering to help Cass pack her things and get dressed for the plane trip. Dorothy sent her away. *She* would take care of everything and choose her mother's traveling outfit. That way, the last word would be hers.

The trip from Boston to Los Angeles with Cass was one of the most memorable journeys I've ever made.

I quickly realized I'd never traveled alone with someone quite so frail and slow-moving. It took Cass so long to walk from her room in the retirement home to the cab waiting at the curb, and from where the cab let us off in front of the terminal to the passenger gate, that we missed our plane. I learned there was only one more flight west, and it had been canceled because too many of the flight crew had called in sick and the airline couldn't staff it. I thought, "God help us, Cass and I are going to have to spend the night in the airport."

Fate took pity. Flight attendants waiting on standby, hoping to ride as nonrevenue passengers to the West Coast in time for New Year's, offered their services for the flight. Not knowing they were going to be pressed into service, a few had had some holiday libation. It wasn't going to be your run-of-the-mill Boston–Los Angeles flight.

Once we were airborne, Cass turned to me tentatively and asked, "Is it all right for me to have a drink? Sort of a farewell to Mr. Barleycorn?"

I said, "Cass, if that's what you need, go right ahead."

Her faded blue eyes began to sparkle.

When the stewardess came with the drink cart, Cass ordered a double Manhattan with two cherries, and opening her purse, asked, "How much is that?"

The young woman smiled. "This is kind of a special flight. Because we were delayed two hours in Boston and because it's so close to New Year's, all drinks are free this evening."

Cass looked like she'd been handed a pass to paradise. Raising her glass to the stewardess, she said, "Then bombs away, my dear."

Buoyed up by Manhattans, Cass became an animated traveling companion. But I was also aware of the physical effects alcohol was having on her. Her tolerance had peaked and then diminished, so now one drink would do what five used to. Her eyes became glassy, her skin ruddy. Talkative, uninhibited, her words slurred, she described her twenty-year career as a travel agent, said she'd visited some of the world's most exotic places. Watching her smiling face, I could glimpse the charming woman she must have been. She confided that once when she was visiting India, a Bengal Lancer had asked for her hand in marriage, and I didn't doubt it for a minute.

At one point, she looked thoughtfully around at her fellow passengers—all celebrating—and then said, "You know, Eddie, compared to the other drunks on this plane, I don't think I'm that bad of a boozer. What do you think?"

I laughed. "Well, Cass, I take them one at a time, and right now I'm concentrating on you."

She laughed too, and said, "That calls for a refill."

But as she started on her next double Manhattan, I began to worry a little. Slow-moving as she'd been in Boston when she was relatively sober, what would she be like when we landed in Los Angeles? How would I get her to my car in the parking lot?

I asked one of the stewardesses to call ahead for a wheelchair. The young woman promised she would, but since she was enjoying this flight as much as the passengers, my faith in her promise was shaky.

However, when we landed in L.A., the wheelchair was there. I put Cass into it and whisked her to the baggage claim area. I said, "Promise me you'll stay put while I go get my car."

She twinkled at me. "But Eddie, where could I go?"

Half an hour later, we were on the freeway bound for the treatment center.

Saying goodbye to Cass in the lobby, I felt as close to her as if we really were related.

"Cass," I said, grinning, "you have a happy new year."

"Eddie," she answered, "I just might do that. Will you come and visit me?"

"I will," I said. And I did.

The last time I saw her, she'd made excellent progress toward recovery. I told her, "Cass, that was the best New Year's Eve I ever spent with anybody."

She winked. "A real high point, eh, Eddie? And who could be higher than I was?"

"Absolutely no one." I kissed her cheek. "You know, I'm not going to forget you."

"Aw, I bet you say that to all the lushes."

"No, I don't. Bet on it. I'll remember you, Cass."

And I have.

Friends and Neighbors

*For it is one of the main duties
of friends to help one another to
be better persons: one must hold
up a standard for one's friend
and be able to count on a true
friend to do likewise. One has to
forgive and indeed, forgiveness
. . . is the very mark of true love
and friendship. But to forgive is
not to excuse. Forgiveness and
the struggle . . . to exemplify the
good go hand in hand.*

ROBERT N. BELLAH, RICHARD MADSEN,
WILLIAM M. SULLIVAN, ANN SWIDLER,
STEVEN M. TIPTON
Habits of the Heart:
Individualism and
Commitment in American Life

Very often, ties relatives attempt to sustain with an addicted family member diminish as parents age or grow ill, siblings move away, and spouses become unable or unwilling to continue devoting emotional or physical energy to the addicted person.

And addicted individuals themselves, because of their dependency on drugs, frequently put distance between themselves and others.

Who, then, will help?

I have led many interventions initiated by people who were not related and sometimes not even emotionally close to the addicted person. These interventions were made possible by what I have come to think of as "commitment to caring." It may have its roots in times past, when connections between people were easier to establish and nurture. Regardless, I encounter it in unexpected places among people who help others out of a sense of mutuality that candidly acknowledges their own vulnerability.

I touched on that kind of caring briefly in Cass Bixby's story. I'm convinced the old gentleman who approached Cass's son, Ted, would, if there had been no family member available, have found a way to aid Cass with the help of the other people living in the retirement home. I could tell in the brief time I worked with them that they, by themselves, after preparation, would have been able to sustain an intervention.

There have also been times when just one person's commitment to caring was enough.

Walter and Sal

Sal was—and had been for twenty years—the manager of an apartment house in downtown San Pedro. Her tenants were mostly middle-aged men who worked on the waterfront. Although she kept track of their comings and goings, she didn't intrude in their lives unless she believed there was an urgent need.

She felt that urgency when she called me about Walter, a widower in his late fifties who had been living in Sal's apartment house for several years. Sal told me Walter's excessive drinking had driven away his children and had probably also contributed to the injury he'd suffered a few months earlier. Working as a warehouseman, he'd driven a forklift into a loading platform.

But even after he recovered from his injury, Walter didn't go back to work. Dipping into his savings when his disability payments ended, he stayed in his apartment, which was directly above Sal's, and had liquor delivered daily. Sal would hear him stumbling and cursing at all hours. A few times, when it sounded like he'd fallen and there was complete silence afterward, she'd knocked on his door and when there was no answer had used her passkey to enter his apartment and found him passed out on the couch or floor.

"A lot of unhappy men live in this building," she told me. "Some of them, you know, they wear depression like their skivvies, shed it only on Saturdays and sometimes not even then. But there was something about Walter. When he was on his feet, he tried to cheer people up, and usually could. I remember one Thanksgiving he rented an Indian costume and went from door to door handing out bags of popcorn." She smiled at the memory, then went on, "I checked with one of his cronies. The warehousemen's union has an insurance plan that would cover the cost of treatment. What do you think? Could we try and get him in?"

I asked Sal if Walter tended to be violent, or if he had any weapons in his apartment.

Sal said he was too ill to be feisty and he just wasn't the type to possess weapons.

So I said, "Sure, then let's go for it."

Since there wasn't anybody to prepare for Walter's intervention, Sal and I agreed we'd intervene early the next morning, the time when his alcohol level would probably be the lowest. I contacted a facility within the area to arrange preadmittance, and the welfare officer of Walter's union to confirm union protocol.

Walking with Sal down the corridor of that old apartment building early the following day spun me back in time to the boardinghouse my grandmother ran after my grandfather died of alcoholism (*my* genetic link to addiction). There was the same boiled-cabbage/oniony/wet-wool smell buildings that are never renovated get.

Walter's apartment was on the second floor. Sal knocked. No answer. She knocked again, waited, then opened the door with her passkey, and we went inside.

"There he is," she said.

I wondered, there who is? A body was lying on the couch with a sheet over its head.

Sal went to the window and raised the shade. Morning sunlight poured into the room.

I slowly drew back the sheet and saw a wasted man curled up in a fetal position.

He winced, opened his eyes, saw me, and said in a foggy voice, "Jesus God, who are you and what are you doing here?"

I believed I had come to a lost cause, but I went ahead and told him what I was there for.

I didn't think he was listening, just supposed he was lying

still and being quiet because that was all he had the strength to do.

But when I stopped talking, he said, "I drink because of the pain."

"What pain?" I asked.

"Ulcers."

I said, "Drinking causes ulcers. It's dangerous to drink if you have ulcers."

He said, "I have other problems."

"Walter," I replied, "everyone who drinks gives me a reason why. I haven't heard one yet that justified throwing a life away."

He blinked at me, owl-like, then said, "Excuse me, I'm going to the bathroom."

I doubted he could sit up, let alone get off that couch and walk. But moving one bone at a time, he got up, hobbled down the hallway to the bathroom, went in, and closed the door.

The apartment was small and the walls were thin. I stood listening to the water run. Sal and I exchanged a look.

Then the damnedest thing happened. Walter came back. He'd washed his face, combed his hair, brushed his teeth.

I asked, "What's up, Walter?"

He said, "Hell, you didn't expect me to go with you looking like that, did you?"

Stunned into a moment of silence, I recovered quickly, told him he'd made a wise decision, and off we went to the treatment center.

I ran into him on the street a year later. I wouldn't have recognized him if he hadn't come up and reintroduced himself. He didn't look anything like the skeleton person I'd seen on that couch. But something had still been alive in him that wanted to be reached, and thanks to Sal, it had been. If she hadn't cared enough to act, Walter would probably have died alone in that apartment.

Recluses. Addiction nurtures isolation, makes hermits out

of all kinds of people who, if they didn't have this terrible disease, wouldn't shut the world away.

Carole Ward

Through my involvement with Carole Ward and several others in the motion-picture industry, I've become aware of the unique and strong commitment to caring that exists among the craftspeople who labor behind the scenes of "the movies." Many families working in the industry occupy the same houses for decades in the San Fernando Valley towns of Burbank, Studio City, Van Nuys, Sherman Oaks.

Carole, age thirty-three, lived alone in the house she had been born in within a couple of miles of the motion-picture studio where her father had worked as a set designer, and where Carole now worked as a wardrobe assistant.

Maybe in a more mobile neighborhood, people wouldn't have come together to help Carole. But Carole's neighbors had known her since childhood, had shared movie gossip with Carole's parents over their backyard fences and had witnessed the young woman's descent into acute alcoholism.

A character actor (whose face most people recognize but whose name they can never remember) lived next door to Carole. He had participated in a stormy intervention I'd done on a scriptwriter a couple of years earlier. He called me about Carole, and said, "Ed, sometimes my wife and I hear her screaming at night."

My instinctive conclusion was DTs—delirium tremens, an acute mental disturbance marked by anxiety and mental distress. It's a form of alcoholic psychosis ordinarily seen after withdrawal from extremely heavy alcohol intake. If Carole was suffering from DTs, she was probably alternating between very heavy binge drinking and periods of remorse and guilt when she tried to stop. But that was speculation on my part.

The minus side of interventions initiated by people who

aren't emotionally involved with the addicted person is that they're often aware of only the exteriors of the addicted person's life and can give me no real insight into current habits, even the severity of addiction. Consequently, I have a far greater sense of venturing into the unknown than I do with family or workplace interventions.

The plus side of these interventions is that there aren't any intrafamily conflicts or pathology to deal with. Everyone who participates does so out of a pure desire to help.

As I expected, Carole's neighbors were able to tell me much more about her past than her present. Carole's parents had wanted her to become an actress, and as a child and adolescent, she was always going to dancing, elocution, and acting classes. She'd had some small parts in movies in her teens, and was beginning to be well reviewed as a stage actress with a local repertory group when her father became gravely ill with Hodgkin's disease. When he died, Carole sought and found emotional release in the Hollywood drug scene. She'd ended up in the hospital close to death herself. After that, she didn't try to act any more. She accepted a job as an assistant wardrobe mistress, lived with her mother, and drank. Her mother suffered several strokes and had died a few years ago.

When Carole's neighbor called me, Carole was on layoff—a blight that periodically afflicts every craft guild in Holly-wood. The actor told me that whenever Carole didn't have to go to work, she slept all day and drank all night, and that was when they'd hear her screaming.

In the years since Carole's mother had died, he and his wife and the neighbors on the other side had issued social invitations to the young woman, which she invariably re-fused. However, his wife had contacted a man who had once been a close family friend of the Wards, and he and his wife both believed Carole would attend a neighborhood gathering if she was told this man was going to be present.

We agreed to intervene at 4:00 on a Tuesday afternoon,

which, for Carole, would be the equivalent of the early-morning hour I'd chosen for Walter, the time when her alcohol level was apt to be the lowest.

Preparation of the other neighbors was swift and clean and accomplished by phone calls. They all agreed on the urgent need for Carole to be physically stabilized, then counseled and educated about her disease of addiction. An excellent treatment center supported by her union was chosen, and admittance arrangements were made.

The quiet street Carole lived on was lined with magnolia trees as old as the house. Trumpet and wisteria vines sprawled over the rooftops.

I arrived at the actor's home where the intervention was going to be held a little before 3:00, wanting to spend some time unifying the group and also to talk to Stewart, the once-close friend of Carole's family. I rang the doorbell, then glanced over at Carole's house. It badly needed painting. Venetian blinds yellowed with age shuttered the windows.

The actor came to the door, welcomed me into his home, and introduced me to the other neighbors and Stewart, a man in his late seventies, about the age Carole's father would have been if he'd lived. Stewart had extraordinary eyes, a bright, twinkling blue, surrounded by a meshwork of wrinkles. In frail health, he lived in a retirement home in the heart of Hollywood.

Stewart told me he'd often worked as a cameraman on the same movies Carole's father had designed sets for. He said, "When I first met the Wards, they had everything. Phil was brilliant, and sought-after. Irene was as beautiful as any movie star, and in fact had been asked to make a screen test. But she had no aspirations of her own; her life revolved around Phil first, and Carole second.

"I was close to all the Wards, but especially Carole. She was one of those youngsters you could relate to without the disparity in age making a bit of difference. I didn't have any kids of my own, so she and I became best friends. We were both fond of 'critters,' loved going to the zoo. We promised we'd always watch out for each other.

"We did, too, for a long time. After her mother's death, Carole started sculpting. The guts and style that had been apparent in her acting began to show up in her work. But then, little by little, the drinking began to eat all that up. When she stopped sculpting, I think she knew she was quitting on herself. It was a bad time. Even I couldn't reach her."

Four o'clock had come and gone while Stewart and I talked, and the neighbors tried not to keep constant watch out the windows. It was almost 4:45 when one of them said, "She's coming." Conversation in the room came to a halt. The doorbell rang, and Carole was ushered into the living room.

She was a pale, fragile-looking woman carrying far too much weight on her small bones—but it wasn't dense weight, it was alcohol bloat. And it hadn't completely hidden the gamine face or the acute intelligence in her eyes.

Those eyes sought and found Stewart, and she moved toward him quickly. He gave her a long, silent hug.

The neighbors then formed a circle around them, and Stewart introduced me. I told Carole what I was there for, and as I spoke, I had the feeling I was being listened to intently.

I said, "Carole, if this meeting accomplishes nothing else, it will make you know you are not alone. Every person in this room cares and is deeply concerned about you.

"I have to say some hard things, because you have a serious, progressive disease that's destroying your life. I know you've suffered a lot of pain, and you drink to sedate yourself to keep from feeling any more. But you're not just anesthetizing the pain. You're deadening your creativity and your capacity for friendship. We want you to get help, Carole. We want you to go into treatment today."

A small frown creased her brow, and she shook her head.

"I have to stay in my house. I can't sleep anywhere but my own house."

Knowing it probably was the only place she felt really safe, I was about to address that when Stewart said softly, "I kept coming to your house, Carole. I must have knocked on your door a hundred times. Nobody ever answered. I called you on the phone—no answer there either. Finally, I gave up. God, I'd like to help you now. If you go into treatment, I promise you I'll come and visit you every day. Shoot, I don't have anybody to go to the zoo with. I miss you like hell."

Their eyes locked. It was one of those moments when the arrow was in flight. Carole would either leave and disappear back inside that haunted house—or she would move into the circle of Stewart's arms.

She pulled her eyes away, said, "I can't."

"Wrong," Stewart responded, and reaching out, took her hand.

A sliver of a second later, her face was pressed against his chest.

She went into treatment that night.

I kept track of her progress in the weeks that followed. The treatment center's staff told me Stewart, true to his promise, visited her every day visiting was allowed.

Not long ago, I was in Carole's neighborhood again and drove down her street. Her house was painted a soft gray. The yellowed venetian blinds had been replaced by wooden shutters and they were open to let in the light.

I wish I could say commitment to caring always works, but I can't.

BEST FRIENDS

In a case I had not long ago, a young man asked me to intervene with his best friend who was heavily addicted to "crack."

123

Crack is a potent, smokable form of cocaine that has become the current drug craze among young adults. It's made by adding baking soda and water to powdered cocaine, heating the mixture until the water has boiled off, letting the mixture cool and cohere, then chopping it into small pellets called "freebase rocks" or "crack."

Powdered cocaine addicts turn to crack because they think it's cheaper—which it isn't. Five dollars buys a rock good for about a ten-minute high, whereas a full gram of powdered cocaine, which sells for seventy-five to one hundred dollars, will keep two users high for an evening.

Also, ironically, "needle-drug" addicts turn to crack because they're afraid of being contaminated with the AIDS virus. But crack is an even faster route to the morgue. It's often blended with harmful ingredients. When it's smoked, high concentrations of it reach the brain in seconds, giving an intense euphoric peak, followed rapidly by a crash into depression. The user craves more crack to escape. The roller-coaster ups and downs make smoking crack five times as addictive as snorting powdered cocaine, and the risks of cardiac arrest, stroke, and seizures are comparably greater.

The friend told me that shortly after becoming addicted, the young addict had moved from southern California to Fort Worth, Texas, to live with a cousin. The friend intended to fly to Texas, gather the cousin and close family members for an early-morning pre-preparation meeting in a Fort Worth hotel, and have the large-group preparation meeting an hour later, after which the cousin would bring the addict to the hotel room for the intervention. The intervention couldn't be held at the condominium where the young man lived with his cousin, because the addict kept several weapons in his bedroom.

It sounded like a pretty shaky plan to me. But I was beginning to know the devastating potency of crack by then. And interventionists have to find their way with new addictive substances just as medical practitioners do.

I asked the young man what his friend did in Fort Worth.

He gave me a wry smile, and said, "Not very much."

I inquired if his friend's family was providing financial aid, and he nodded.

"Enough to support his habit?" I asked.

"No. Just enough to keep him out of their lives. Food, clothing, rent. That's it."

So whatever the addict was doing to obtain money to buy crack was undoubtedly illicit.

The friend flew to Fort Worth as planned, but the addict, suspecting something was afoot, would have nothing to do with him.

I arrived a few days later. Even though I intuited that the cousin the young man was living with might not be trustworthy, the pre-preparation with close family members went fairly well. But within the first ten minutes of the larger group meeting, I sensed intense antipathy among the more distant family. They hadn't come out of a desire to help the crack addict, but to find a way to stop the drain he was making on the family's financial resources. I offered to abort the intervention, but the friend pleaded with the family to go through with it, and they assented.

The cousin left at 11:30 to get the young man. Keeping the others calm was like trying to hold marbles in a straight line.

At five minutes past noon, the hotel-room door flew open and the addict stood glaring in at all of us, his eyes wild. He said his cousin had told him what we were planning, then he shouted he owned a machine gun and if anyone came after him, he wouldn't hesitate to use it. With that, he turned and ran down the hotel corridor.

The friend and I followed as the young man disappeared through a door marked "Stairs." By the time we opened it, he was two flights below us, taking the steps three at a time.

When I said there was no point in going after him, I saw the look in his friend's eyes I'd seen in other interventions that had gone awry—a desperate urgency to reclaim a loved one from hell. Gently, I told him the addicted person had to be reachable. If someone runs away, there's nothing I can do except help those involved with that person accept what has happened.

I used everything I knew in order to release that young man from further involvement with his friend's acute chemical dependency. During my last hour with him, I asked him to write a letter to his friend, telling him how much he cared and wanted him to get help. I put the letter in a large envelope and arranged for it to be hand-delivered. It was after midnight when I flew out of Forth Worth.

I found out a year later that the crack addict had admitted himself to a county facility for six months' extended treatment, and that the prognosis for his recovery was guarded.

Cocaine and its derivatives put people closer to the abyss than any other drug. And though I will intervene using the caring commitment of just one person, when cocaine is the drug involved, I yearn for a whole community of caring. Which is just what I got with Milo Visotti.

Milo

Stopping by my office late one Thursday evening on my way home from an intervention, I saw a call slip with a bright red V for "Very Urgent" Olive had taped to my telephone. There was a note at the bottom that the caller, Randy Visotti, had gotten my name from Phil Rolley.

Phil was a rancher I'd intervened with for alcoholism about six months previously. He lived in a rich agricultural farming valley several hundred miles to the north. Labor problems and low crop prices had depressed the economy in that valley, and excessive use of cocaine and alcohol among the ranchers was escalating.

When Phil's wife had asked me to intervene with him, she'd said his disposition had become so erratic that something as small as a picture hanging crooked could set him off. So the morning I walked into their house, I expected an explosion. Instead, calm and grimly resigned, Phil agreed to go to a treatment center. And he'd done well, too. I'd spoken to him a few weeks before and he told me he'd celebrated his fifth month of sobriety. "The economy hasn't gotten any better," he said, "but my ability to cope with it has."

We'd talked a little about the escalating addiction problem in that depressed valley.

Phil said, "I thought drinking was a way to not think about the damn market. But I learned in treatment that blaming bad times for my drinking was just a way to deny my illness. All my life I'd found excuses to drink.

"Thing is, there are a whole lot of people in this valley using the market as an excuse. Guys who wouldn't normally booze it up or snort cocaine are trying it. And some are getting in deep trouble."

I dialed the number on the call ship. Randy Visotti thanked me for returning his call and said, "I need to talk to you about my brother, Milo." I heard desperation in his voice and asked what was going on.

Randy told me that four years ago when their father died, Milo, as eldest son, in accordance with their Swiss family tradition had been named heir to the 119-acre Visotti ranch. He said he and Milo had never been close, in fact, had disagreed on just about everything since childhood He knew if he stayed on at the ranch, he would have ideas that differed from Milo's about how to revitalize the land, which had been neglected during their father's long illness. So he'd accepted a job as a farm technician with a fertilizer firm and moved to the opposite end of the valley. As time passed, he'd sensed things weren't going well for his brother, but had not interfered until Milo's best friend, Ramon Garcia, called to tell him he'd better get home, that Milo was so deep into cocaine he was in danger of losing the ranch.

Randy went home, talked to several neighbors and local

merchants, and inspected the ranch books one afternoon. He discovered his brother had been taking money from crop sales, as well as checks the bank issued to him to purchase equipment and supplies, to buy cocaine. He'd been using at a rapidly escalating rate for three years and wasn't even going to be able to harvest the crops he presently had in the ground because word had gone around among migrant ranch laborers not to work for Milo. Also the utility companies had given notice they were going to close the ranch down.

By the time Randy finished telling me his brother's story, I sensed Randy's deep anger at the threatened loss of the ranch. I'd also received the impression there wasn't anyone in the valley Milo hadn't lied to or betrayed. So I wondered who would be willing to participate in an intervention and whether there was anyone left who could still reach Milo on a feeling level. I doubted Randy could. As he'd said, he and Milo had never been close, and Randy's anger was sealing off any fraternal feeling that might have existed.

Perhaps their mother?

Randy said, "No, since my dad's death, with her diabetes and all, she just isn't strong enough. I don't want her involved."

"Well, I'm going to need people Milo will listen to," I told him.

"I know. I've been working on it." He named several men of the valley who had agreed to take part. Phil Rolley was one, and I was glad to hear it. People who have been intervened with and have made good progress are often powerful in interventions; they can be a strong testimonial.

Randy said he wanted to get Milo into treatment as quickly as possible so he could straighten things out with the bank and try to save the land. He asked how soon I could come to the valley.

I told him I could fly up Sunday for the preparation and we could intervene Monday morning.

Because the men he wanted to participate lived in towns all over the valley, I agreed to hold the preparation meeting in the motel I'd be staying at, which was in a central location. Randy said he'd see me there at 2:00 on Sunday afternoon.

Scanning my notes after I hung up, I decided it was a small miracle Milo had survived.

I think of cocaine (and crack) as "leapfrog" drugs. With alcohol, it can take a person years to reach the severe, life-threatening stage (which is probably one of the reasons our culture has legitimated it). But with cocaine and its derivatives, a person can be totally dependent in weeks. Also psychotic.

Although I look forward to persuading cocaine addicts to take the first step toward recovery, I'm always aware of the paranoia caused by cocaine. It can make my work extremely difficult and sometimes impossible. I hoped Randy would be successful in gathering a strong group of men.

Three days later, I was sitting in front of a motel-room window in Arroyo Verde listening to the wind blow. I'd been to that valley enough times to know the wind would die tonight and then tomorrow would come up again.

I had the door of the motel room open, and flies were coming in. I felt incredibly lonely and didn't know why exactly. Maybe because I was tired, or the weekend before was one of those rare ones I'd been able to spend with my family and I wished I were with them now; or maybe because Randy had said he'd meet me at 2:00, and was already an hour late, and for all I knew might have decided not to come at all. At 3:30, he still hadn't shown up, and I couldn't help thinking how much of what I do is based on trust in strangers. After telephone conversations with people I don't know, I board planes and trains, travel to out-of-the-way places, then check into a hotel. And I wait.

Another half hour passed. My apprehension grew.

Finally a pickup truck pulled up in front of my motel unit.

Through the window, I studied the young man who got out of the truck. He was short and stocky, and moved quickly. I opened the door. "Randy?"

He nodded. "Sorry for being so late. Milo took off for a '49er game in Frisco this morning, so I was out at the ranch trying to straighten things out and lost track of the time." His dark brown hair was straight, the hazel eyes direct. He looked exhausted.

Leaning against the pickup, he kicked some mud off his boots, saying since he'd talked to me on Thursday he'd been through the books again. "Our land is probably worth close to half a million, and we're down about half. I went to the bank as soon as they opened their doors last Friday and asked for a loan so I could get our fuel pumps going. They said they'd grant it if Milo was off the ranch. I figure the reason they were willing to go along with me is that they've already taken so much land from people around here going bankrupt, they decided it was better business to let me try and get the crops in."

He shook his head. "Thing is, Milo was running around higher than a kite during planting season and didn't push the water through far enough. A third of the land is barren. I didn't tell the guys at the bank that."

I asked him to come inside, and we sat and talked about the ranch a little more. Then he said, "The men who want to help Milo have agreed to come here tonight around seven, if that's okay with you."

"That's fine."

Briefly, he told me about them: Ramon Garcia, Milo's friend who had called Randy to tell him the ranch was in danger. Milo and Ramon had gone through elementary and high school together. Tom Alvarez, a patriarchal figure in the community who had acted as a father figure to Randy and Milo after their own father died.

"And you already know Phil Rolley."

I nodded.

The last was Calvin Lima, Milo's former business partner, who, after the breakup of their partnership, had become one of the most respected ranchers in the valley.

"Cal does it right," Randy said. "Gets peak prices for his crops, is liked by his workers, has a beautiful wife, two great kids. Milo knows it could have been that way for him, too."

Hearing a bitter tone, I said, "Randy, do you think you can speak to your brother without letting your anger about what's happened to the ranch show?"

He looked out the window for a minute, then shook his head. "Nope."

"Your presence is going to be important," I told him. "But it might be best if you limit your comments to your family's pride and that you'll be involved in his treatment during the intervention."

He nodded, got up, said he had to go back out to the ranch and get as much done as he could while Milo was in San Francisco, and he'd see me at the motel again in a few hours.

After he left, I sat thinking about how to structure the intervention. I sensed the men's concern would be deep, because as Phil and I had discussed, what was happening to Milo was happening to many others threatened by shifting markets, rising labor costs, trouble with unions, and the complexities of mechanization—and, starting in the late 1970s, the cocaine epidemic. Offered a white powder that would block out their worries with euphoria, many young ranchers tried it—and many, like Milo, couldn't stop.

But it didn't seem likely any of the men Randy had described would hold real power over his brother. I would just have to hope that because Milo was of "the arroyo," these men cared about him enough to reach him.

I had two hours before they would all gather in my motel room, and the familiar what-shall-I-do-to-pass-the-time feeling came over me.

Arroyo Verde is only about eight blocks long. Earlier, I'd noticed a cross on top of a church steeple at the opposite end

131

of town, so I decided I'd walk over and light a candle for Milo.

Starting down the town's main street, I had to bend my head against that nerve-rasping wind that seemed as though it might be a close relative of the Santa Ana that blows where I live.

The church was a small stucco building with wooden doors painted bright blue. The cross atop its peaked roof was strung with Christmas lights that looked left over from last year (maybe even the year before). A sign in front told me the church was named Trinitas, and that made me feel less like a stranger, because my own church in San Pedro is named Holy Trinity.

It was cool and peaceful inside. The light was dim. There wasn't anyone else there, probably because it was close to the ranchers' supper hour. Beneath the high beamed ceiling, stained-glass windows were set in the walls, and late-afternoon sun coming through those windows cast colored squares of light on the wooden floor. Wrought-iron stands on either side of the altar held votive candles. A sign hand-lettered in a child's large printing said: "10-hour lights—20 cents." It seemed like such a bargain, I lit a candle for Milo and for each of the men who were going to be present. I knelt in front of the altar and asked for help—for the men tomorrow, for myself to find the right words, and most of all, for Milo to hear us.

Then I walked back to the motel. While I waited for Randy and the others, I went to the soft-drink machine near the office, putting in enough coins to get four soft drinks out of it. I'd done enough interventions in this valley to know ranchers like something in their hands. They look at what they hold while they listen to you, thinking about what you've said.

Tom Alvarez was the first to arrive. He had gray hair and strong age lines in his face, and he introduced himself solemnly.

Between 7:00 and 7:15, three more pickup trucks, including Randy's, parked out front.

Sitting close to the window, Tom Alvarez was the first to tell me a little about himself; for instance, that he now owned the town's oldest market, where he'd started out clerking as a boy. But very soon, he was talking about his relationship with the Visottis. "I've known Milo and Randy since the day they were born. I helped their father shingle the walls of the house they grew up in, drank wine at their christenings and watched them turn into men.

"But things have changed here since old Visotti and I were young. The army base nearby keeps growing bigger and they don't have enough housing for the soldiers, so what do they do? Build up our little ranching community with double-decker apartments and cheap tracts. Even a shopping center north of town. You'll find the stores there selling things people around here don't want. Mr. Storti, I feel we are not any more what we should be, and maybe that's one reason so much cocaine is coming into our valley."

Gazing out the motel-room window, Tom told me how four years ago he'd acted as confidant to Milo when the young man took over the family ranch. "He trusted me then," Tom said. "But since the cocaine—I don't know if he does anymore. He's very different."

Listening to Tom, studying him, I thought he might be my power person, capable of reaching Milo, making him listen.

Ramon Garcia sat opposite Tom. Randy had told me Ramon was successful, owned acres of land in both Mexico and Arroyo Verde. He was a dark-skinned, heavyset young man who didn't want to meet my eyes. Then he said something that startled us. "I was the one who introduced Milo to cocaine," he confessed.

The men gave him quick, sharp glances.

Then Tom Alvarez touched the younger man's arm.

And after a few seconds, Randy said, "If it hadn't been you, Ray, it would have been someone else."

"Yeah, well, I keep remembering it." He sighed and moved his shoulders as if trying to shift a burden that had been there a long time. "We were driving to Monterey in my old pickup and a radiator hose blew out. There wasn't any way we could fix it until the next day, so we had a whole damn night to kill. We were on a back road. I had a six-pack of beer in the truck, some pot, a gram of cocaine.

"In those days, coke was still a novelty, something a lot of guys fooled around with. But I remember Milo didn't want to try it. He kept saying, 'No, Ray, I don't think so.' Then after the beer and pot were gone, I said, 'Come on, Milo, what's it going to hurt?' And he finally did. Afterward he asked, 'So what's the big deal? I didn't feel much.' But a month later, he was buying. He never stopped."

I could tell from the expression in Ramon's dark eyes how much he blamed himself, and I believed his presence, his sympathy, would be important.

Phil Rolley was the second-oldest man there. He was wiry, freckled, with ginger-colored sideburns and mustache. He couldn t sit still, kept getting up, pacing, then sitting down again. I suspected it was because the memory of his own intervention was still so raw.

He said, "Damn cocaine is all over the arroyo now. It comes down here from San Jose and Monterey, up from Mexico, over from Soledad. In the beginning, you'd hear, 'Cocaine doesn't hurt you. Try some. It makes you feel great.' But now we know coke's worse than heroin. It's the most addictive drug there is.

"And there's no damn respect with cocaine. For instance, my friends knew I went to a treatment center, so when I got back to town, I told them I was through drinking and not one of them invited me to have a drink. But my son was on cocaine for a while. He had a hell of a time. Coke users don't care if you went to a treatment program, they're still going to ask, 'Hey, do you want some coke? Come on!' So it's going to be hard for Milo."

Calvin Lima nodded at the things Phil was saying. Milo's ex-partner was over six feet tall, with strong features, dark-blond hair, serious eyes. Like the others, he'd grown up in the valley, but hadn't known Milo well until the two entered agricultural college the same year. Then they became good friends. "Just something about Milo kind of balanced out with me," Calvin recalled. "I'm tall, he's short; I'm lean, he's heavy; I'm serious, he jokes around. We just fit together. So when Milo was called back here because his father was dying, I decided to come home, too.

"I knew Milo didn't have much in the way of equipment to work his ranch, and because I had access to a lot through my family—well, that's how we became partners.

"After a couple of years, I decided we could expand, but Milo had started to pull away by then, gave me some crap about not wanting more responsibility.

"The day our partnership ended, I went out to the Visotti ranch to talk to him. You know—try to get him to change his mind. I remember when he saw me, he didn't come forward. In fact, he turned away. And something in the way he did that, stiff as a fence, not looking at me or talking much, made me face what I hadn't before: not simply that the partnership was over, but something else was way off base.

"After that, I tried to get him to talk to me once or twice, not about business, just about himself. What was happening, what he thought, stuff like that. But he avoided me."

Randy said, "Every time he saw you he had to face what he'd lost." Again, I heard the bitter echo and believed Randy was talking about his own feelings, too.

"Maybe," Calvin said. "The thing that's haunted me is, if I hadn't been so damned ambitious, maybe I could have helped him."

I tried to ease him. "You couldn't. The only thing that would have helped Milo was to get off cocaine."

Listening to the men, observing them, I could tell that with the exception of Phil, they were uncomfortable because we

135

would be taking Milo by surprise tomorrow. I'd encountered that same apprehension in other interventions I'd done in the valley. So I addressed it, told them my experience had taught me that if Milo knew in advance about the intervention, he'd never show up. The element of surprise, I assured them, was for Milo's benefit.

After a while, they seemed to accept that, saying they would do their best the next morning. I had found in them, as I had hoped, a deep concern for the man.

We set 6:00 A.M. as the time for the intervention. After the men left, I couldn't help remembering Randy had mentioned Milo kept a shotgun collection in an outbuilding adjacent to the Visotti house, and was an excellent marksman. When I know there are firearms accessible to an addicted person, I ask a family member to take the bullets out of the guns. But Randy told me Milo had the only key to the outbuilding.

I didn't sleep—I never do sleep much before an intervention. Especially when I'm dealing with cocaine, I keep going over the case to unravel any flaws prior to going in.

So I was up, ready and waiting at 5:00 A.M. when Randy arrived in his truck. Calvin Lima was with him. It was dark out, the kind of dark you get in these small valley towns where there are no streetlights or neon signs. And quiet. I'm used to the predawn bustle of truckers heading for the freeway, city refuse trucks making their rounds. Here— nothing.

I sat between the two men as we drove down the main street of Arroyo Verde. They wore plaid flannel shirts and jeans. I was in a blue suit, white shirt, and tie. Even when I'm with ranchers, I don't dress casually for an intervention, because I don't take it casually.

My foot touched something on the floor, and bending over, I saw a gun case. Randy reached across, picked it up, put it behind the seat, murmured, "Sorry. I carry a gun because Milo owes his dealers money, and I figure they might come after me."

When we drove by Tom Alvarez's market, he pulled out behind us in his pickup, and later, as we turned onto Yucaipa Way, the narrow road leading to the ranch, Ramon Garcia and Phil Rolley were waiting in another truck to fall in line.

As we drove down Yucaipa, the windows in a few of the ranch houses were lit. I stared at those lighted windows, almost convincing myself I could smell sausage and bacon frying, because everything else I might have focused on—the black, silent trees, the dark houses where no one was up, the fences, the narrow road itself—seemed pretty grim.

After we'd gone a few miles, Randy turned onto an even smaller and deeply rutted road that wound down to the Visotti ranch. The truck bounced so badly I braced myself on the dashboard. When we finally got out in front of the house, the ranch dogs—shut up in the barn—began barking furiously. I didn't see how anyone could sleep through that din. In fact, the whole scene—the dark, the trucks, the barking, the men—reminded me of the kind of drug heist you see on television. So when we entered the house, I was prepared for Milo to be up and demanding to know what the hell was going on.

But he wasn't there.

The living room I followed Randy into reminded me of the one in my Italian-immigrant grandparents' house. The couch and two overstuffed chairs were upholstered in brown mohair, their arms covered with crocheted doilies. The tables were made of old, polished wood; the lamp shades were fringed. I felt as though I'd stepped into another part of the century.

A photograph of a man and woman stood on the mantel above the fireplace: Randy and Milo's parents, I supposed. Old Visotti wore a dark double-breasted suit; she, a full-skirted dress with long sleeves, lace at the collar and cuffs. They stood straight, formal, "posing," the man's fingers touching the woman's.

Next to the picture of the man and woman were high

school photos of Randy and a young man I assumed must be Milo. I looked away quickly. I don't like to see pictures of the person I'm going to intervene with—not only because photographs can be misleading but also because I have to struggle against forming preconceptions anyway.

For example, family members will often describe an addicted person as being equivalent to King Kong because they've given that person power and control over their lives. Yet when I actually meet the person, he or she is more likely to be frail and ill, so I've learned to resist forming any impression at all prior to an intervention.

Randy said he was going to get his brother and went down the hallway.

While he was gone, Tom Alvarez told me in an apologetic tone that he could only stay for an hour, because he had to open his market at 7:00 A.M., sharp.

"But Tom," I said quickly, "sometimes an intervention takes longer than an hour."

He nodded. "I'm sorry." And I sensed all the mornings of his life he must have been there to open those doors at 7:00 A.M.

When I was starting out as an interventionist, I probably would have said, "Hey, Tom, if you can't go the distance, I don't want you to participate." But now I knew I wanted as much time as Tom could give me, because I believed he might be the one person capable of reaching Milo on a feeling level. If Tom left too soon, I'd just have to wing it.

So I said, "Sure, I understand. If you need to leave, just ease your way out."

Randy walked back into the room looking angry. "Dammit! His bed hasn't been slept in. He didn't even come home last night."

The men glanced at each other uneasily.

I asked Randy, "Where do you think he is? Any idea?"

"Well . . . only one place he crashes if he's been partying: Betty's. She's sort of like a cousin. Lives in town."

I said, "Call her, find out if Milo's there. If he is, tell her there's a problem at the ranch and he needs to get out here right now."

Randy shook his head. "He won't care if there's a problem."

I said, "Then tell him it's an emergency."

Randy went into the hallway to make the call.

Meanwhile, I worked at reassuring the men, telling them everything was still going to go well—one delay would not ruin the intervention. But while I was doing this, I kept flashing back on another cocaine addict, a seventeen-year-old girl. Like Milo, she wasn't home at the time set for the intervention. Her distraught father finally tracked her down, phoned her, and told her there was an emergency at home.

I remembered how wired the girl was when she walked in, demanding to know what the emergency was, who I was. I told her I was there to discuss her drug problem. She kicked over a coffee table and screamed at her father.

Then she headed for the kitchen, saying she was going to make herself a sandwich—which is fairly typical behavior. Sometimes people do it to let you know they are in control and you can't boss them around—as Jed O'Brien did when he went into the kitchen to get his cup of coffee. Other times, people just want to be alone to regain their composure.

With this girl, it was sheer defiance.

I followed her into the kitchen, speaking firmly. "Beverly, the sandwich will have to wait."

Her eyes started going back and forth from me to a bread knife on the kitchen table. "*Nobody* tells me what to do." She took a step toward the table.

I held my ground. "Not a good move, Beverly."

She spun around, glared, ran out of the kitchen and down the hall into her bedroom and locked the door. A stereo came on at full volume.

For a moment, I just stood there, grateful she hadn't gone for the knife. Then I walked to the door of her bedroom. However, I took care to stand off to one side so that if she had a gun and shot through the door, she'd miss me. Somehow I was able to talk loudly enough to be heard over the volume of the stereo.

She was listening, because from time to time, she'd respond shrilly, "Get lost, zero man," or "My dealer finds you here, he'll have your eyeballs," followed by high-pitched laughter.

She never did open that door (although her father called me later to tell me she had admitted herself to a treatment center). I left Beverly's house telling myself I would never attempt to intervene again when the person wasn't present at the appointed time.

Yet here I was in Milo Visotti's home in circumstances so similar, I felt seasick.

Randy came back into the living room. "He's at Betty's. They partied after the game. She said she'd get him on his way."

Then he brought the men mugs of coffee from the kitchen.

He offered me some, too, but I said no. When I'm doing an intervention, I don't want any caffeine.

The old pendulum clock on the wall chimed 6:00. The men were sitting where I had told them to, except for Phil, who alternated between sitting and pacing, and Randy, who stood staring out a window. Once he murmured, "Where the hell is he? I think I should go get him."

Waiting is hard. It helps people if I talk them through it. Often that's difficult for me, because what I really want to do is be quiet and prepare myself for what's coming. But I worked at taking the edge off, saying, "Listen, you're all doing the right thing by being here. When Milo comes in, the first three to five minutes, you're going to feel anxious. That's natural. Just stay with your belief in what you're doing for him."

Slowly, as the men started to relax a little, I quieted, easing into a companionable silence.

Just as the sky was beginning to grow light, we heard the

sound of a pickup truck bouncing along the road. It stopped. The truck door opened, then shut. Footsteps moved toward the house. The dogs that had set up such a clamor when we arrived were quiet.

The front door opened. Since the entrance hallway was linoleum, it magnified sound, and the boots I heard clomping created the image of a large, angry man. But the one who appeared and stood staring at us was quite short, with intense, puzzled eyes.

Most cocaine addicts are thin to the point of emaciation, though some remain heavy. Bloated, in fact. Milo's body, his whole posture, reflected the peculiar stress of being overweight and undernourished.

Suddenly Milo reminded me of a young longshoreman I'd worked with, a troubled, ill young man, but a deeply kind one. I've learned to tap into such positive memories, so as warmly as if I were speaking to my long-ago friend, I said, "Hi, Milo, how are you? It's good to meet you. Come on in, sit down over here."

But his eyes left me, moving suspiciously around the circle of men. Focusing on Phil, he swore at him: "You bastard, you set me up. You want to get me in the same place you were in."

Then he turned on me. "I know what you're here for, and you can go to hell!"

I went on as if I hadn't heard, "Why not come and sit over here, next to Tom? We want you to hear about something we've been discussing."

He said, "I don't want any damn thing—except for you to leave my house. That's all! You haven't been asked here."

I disagreed. "I've been asked by your brother and your friends, and I'm not going to leave until you listen to what we have to say. So I'd appreciate it if you would give me a few moments. You know, these men are here because they want to help."

"I don't need it."

Well, I kept talking. It's absolutely vital at a time like that.

I said, "Milo, the people I intervene with have to be special—because I don't just show up. I'm not Santa Claus coming down the chimney. I have to be asked—by people who care."

I gestured. "Look at these men. I worked with them last night, then here in your living room this morning. They're extraordinary people, and all in your corner. Maybe through this addiction you have, you've already accepted the fact that you're going to die. But your friends haven't, I haven't. And we're determined not to lose you."

I thought he was winding down enough to listen, but then he burst out, "You got me here by lying! This isn't an emergency."

"Oh?" I said. "You could have fooled me, because looking at you, we see a dying man. Isn't that an emergency?"

He didn't answer.

I persisted. "Milo?"

"I have to call Betty," he snapped. "She thought it was serious. She'll be worried."

I said, "All right, go call her." As long as he was focusing on someone caring about him, I believed he would be okay. Also, when you're getting close to people like Milo and they're beginning to feel vulnerable, they'll often try to throw a monkey wrench to stop the process. You allow for that and try to give them space and dignity so they don't bolt.

Milo went into the hall, and we heard him pick up the phone. "Betty, listen, it was a false alarm. Yeah, everything's fine."

He reappeared in the arched entrance to the living room. "I'm going to get a cup of coffee."

What I saw in his eyes wasn't defiance but a need for time alone to regain his balance (like Jed O'Brien's wanting to run). So I treated it lightly. "Fine. You get your coffee."

He went down the hallway toward the kitchen.

I was a little uneasy, though. After all, there was a back

door. He could get one of his guns, come back, and order us all out of his house. Or he could just get in his truck and drive away.

But Ramon Garcia said softly, "Milo has never been a morning person. He always feels better after coffee."

I've learned to trust the perceptions of close friends who participate in interventions. While I'm intimate with addiction itself, they know the addicted person's habits and idiosyncrasies better than I do.

So again, we waited.

I listened to the refrigerator door opening, then cupboard doors being opened, too, and shut. After that, silence.

It was probably only a few minutes, but it seemed much longer before Milo came back down the hallway. He stood again in the entrance to the living room, holding his coffee mug, not speaking. Something in his posture told me his resistance had given way to the deep exhaustion he'd been fighting for months.

Again I said, "Sit down, Milo. There, between Tom and Ramon."

Tom touched the empty sofa cushion beside him.

Milo moved toward them like a sleepwalker and sat down. Then Calvin Lima pulled his chair up closer. Soon we had put Milo within the circle of his friends.

I spoke gently. "Milo, at this moment, you're dying."

He answered, "Yeah, I guess."

"Then you know you're addicted."

"Sure."

I smiled. "Well, if you do know that, you've won the first battle. Because acknowledging addiction gives you the chance to do something about it. And right now."

When someone easily admits his or her addiction, it's necessary to present the solution as soon as possible.

While Milo lit a cigarette, and started sucking the smoke in deeply the way addicted people do, I told him things he already knew, but that he needed to hear from a stranger—

a specialist—and I urged him to go into a treatment center today before everything was lost: his ranch, his friends, his life.

He listened and smoked and nodded his head, apparently agreeing.

But I've had people agree with me like that before—especially people who acknowledge their addiction easily. I'll never forget one corporate executive I intervened with, an alcoholic. At every statement I made, he nodded. "You're right. And you know what? You're really good at what you do."

"Thank you," I said. "That's why your firm asked me to talk to you."

But I didn't care if he thought I was good. I wanted him to act on what I was presenting.

The executive said, "I hope you continue with your work, Ed, because you're a master salesman." I tensed, recognizing dismissal, and he went on, "I'm just not buying what you're selling. You see, drinking's the one thing left I'm really good at, because the truth is, I don't care anymore. There's nothing anyone could say to make me change."

When I left him, he was pouring a drink, and he raised his glass to me in a toast. Years earlier, I would have taken my failure to reach him as a personal defeat. But as time passed, I'd seen how in worst-case instances, addiction can create an insanity which puts people out of my reach.

Sitting in Milo's living room, with him nodding and agreeing, I didn't feel especially confident.

So I kept at it. "Milo, I want you to come with me now to the treatment center. All the arrangements have been made."

He stopped agreeing. Staring down at his feet, he told us the reasons he couldn't go. Who would look in on his mother, straighten out his bank accounts, pay his bills, feed the dogs and ducks, harvest the crops and prepare the ground for new crops?

These were things he hadn't been doing anyway. But at least they were objections that could be dealt with.

Instantly, I called on the men to answer him, and they did, each one promising to step in and take care of certain duties.

But even so, he sat on the couch shaking his head.

Tom Alvarez said softly, "Milo, your father would want you to do what Ed's telling you. He'd say the same things."

"I can't," Milo whispered. "I'm in too deep."

I'd been so certain Tom would be able to reach him. My initial fear, that perhaps no one could, returned. I looked around the circle, searching for a "jolt" person, knowing if I didn't make the right choice we might lose this man. It was between Calvin Lima and Ramon Garcia. Perhaps both of them could reach him; perhaps neither.

"Calvin?" I asked.

The young rancher gave me a startled glance, and for a moment he didn't speak. Milo stirred restlessly on the couch, his eyes going toward the door. Slowly Calvin leaned toward his friend, close enough to touch him, and then he did touch him. He gripped Milo's arms tightly in his large hands and said, "The last time I was close enough to touch you, you wouldn't look at me. So I walked away. Just turned and left. But I keep coming back to that moment, time after time. I can't shake it even now, no matter how far away we are. But Milo, you can do something. You can get well and it'll be like it was, I promise. For God's sake, try. Please!"

Milo didn't respond.

Calvin let go of him, put his head down, and covered his face with his hands. He was crying.

Milo drew back, averting his head. He closed his eyes. At last he spoke in a voice so low I almost couldn't hear it. "I'll go."

Nodding at Randy, I quietly instructed him to help Milo pack the clothes he would need.

After they left the room, I glanced over at the pendulum

clock and smiled at Tom. He still had fifteen minutes before he had to open the doors of his market.

He got up to leave, turned. "It was good," he said. "Old Visotti . . ." He didn't finish.

He didn't have to. I knew.

Four of us went with Milo to the treatment center, a ninety-minute drive.

Expressions of fear and doubt kept washing over Milo's face while he lit cigarette after cigarette. As he smoked, I was conscious of his breathing. It was noisy and heavy through his mouth because cocaine had destroyed his nasal membranes.

Once more, I kept the conversation going, but away from his problem this time. I talked about cellular phones in cars, the new fall lineup on TV, upcoming bowl games. The others responded, though we didn't expect Milo to. He was huddled in a dark corner far within himself.

Because I'd been there, I understood how much effort and time it would take for him to come out, and I'd told him that in his living room. But I'd also said that because he had the courage not to die, his life might take on a meaning and purpose he couldn't foresee. It happens. I know.

I kept in close touch with Randy while Milo was in treatment and for several months after he got out. Randy told me, "I thought very seriously about not having Milo take charge of the ranch again. But then I talked to him and I thought, what kind of man would he end up being? That's all he knows. There are restrictions. My name is going to be on every check he signs. That's not because I think he's weak. Cocaine became a disease with Milo, just like diabetes did with my mother. I'm not saying he doesn't have any responsibility for his addiction. He does. But God, it's going to be hard.

"Phil Rolley said to me, 'Randy, the land will always take

you back, and so Milo's going to be okay.' I hope to God he's right."

Milo Visotti stayed straight. He also persuaded two ranchers he once did cocaine with to go into treatment.

Intervention in the Workplace

Labor preserves us from three great evils—weariness, vice, and want.

VOLTAIRE
Candide

W hile interventionists hope people they intervene with will enter treatment motivated by the love and caring expressed by intervention participants, unfortunately that isn't always enough.

Jed O'Brien was surrounded by a loving (albeit damaged) family, but it also took his boss's telling Jed he wasn't performing well on the job to fracture Jed's resistance to going into treatment.

Even in Milo Visotti's intervention, underlying the caring commitment of his friends was the work ethic that existed in that valley where the endeavors of each were tied to the economic good of all.

It's inherent in our culture that part of our sense of self—and for some of us, a substantial part—is defined by the work we do. We use it to assess our worth and give our identity something to hang its hat on. When we are faced with the loss of that index of worth and identity, we feel unmoored, often terrified. That's why workplace interventions initiated by employers and/or associates are practically always successful.

Particularly when someone's job is all she has left.

Ginger and Lorraine

When I arrived at my office a little past noon on a Tuesday after giving a guest lecture at UCLA, Olive handed me my stack of messages and told me she'd put Ginger Nash's number on top—Ginger had called twice from Seattle and wanted me to call her back as soon as I could.

I went into my office, sat down at my desk, and dialed the number. The switchboard operator put me through to Ginger's secretary, who told me "Ms. Nash" was out to lunch and would be in a board conference from 2:00 until 4:00. Would I care to leave a message.

I left my name and said I'd call back, then swung my swivel chair toward the window and sat looking out at the harbor thinking about the last time I'd been with Ginger. We'd done an intervention with a young computer programmer at her firm who was addicted to amphetamines.

Amphetamines can be the chemical of choice for people under intense temporary pressure: students cramming for exams, truck drivers wanting to reach their destination without stopping for sleep, people who have a deadline to meet and are afraid they're not going to make it. As stimulants, amphetamines relieve fatigue, reduce the need for sleep, and produce false feelings of intellectual acuity. Yet used frequently and excessively, they generate dependence, isolation, fear, and sometimes violent behavior, as well as paranoia and possible death from overdose. In general, they are very dangerous.

Working around the clock to solve the intriguing riddles of his computer chips, the programmer had gotten hooked. The intervention had gone smoothly, mainly because of Ginger's clear and spirited message that the young man was an asset to the firm and she did not intend to lose him to a disease that was treatable. The young man did well in treatment and, as far as I knew, was still with the firm.

Ginger's zeal and feistiness were obvious the first time we met—which was before I became an interventionist. Ginger was nineteen then, and an alcoholic. I was counselor-in-charge of the program for chemical-dependent teenagers at Peninsula Hospital. When Ginger entered the program, it was her second time in treatment. The first time she'd admitted herself into a thirty-day residential program, she'd "walked" after two and a half days. She'd acknowledged she had a drinking problem but had stated emphatically that she was not an alcoholic and all she needed to do to stop drinking was change her life-style. She'd checked herself out of the detox unit of the hospital AMA (against medical advice), moved out of her apartment, quit her job, and found a new apartment and job.

Two months later, she entered my group, ready to do whatever she had to do to abstain from drinking and work on her behavior. This time she tackled the hard work of recovery with fierce determination.

Friends she made after she attained sobriety were astonished when she told them she'd been a drunk. "Why?" they asked. "You've got everything. Beauty, brains, talent."

It certainly seemed so.

She'd lived in the same house the first eighteen years of her life, within walking distance of elementary and high schools where she got straight A's. She excelled at her piano and ballet lessons, never went dateless on a Saturday night.

She was strikingly attractive, with taffy-colored hair she wore straight and waist-length. Her strong features, high cheekbones, and cayenne disposition she attributed to her Amerindian great-grandmother.

And yet, despite life's obvious gifts to her, the first time she drank three cans of beer, she said it was like finding the perfect dress, one she'd been looking for all her life and never wanted to take off. She loved the feeling of being intoxicated. It softened the demands she constantly made on herself to be a high achiever, and soon, as she put it, her body and soul demanded the relief alcohol provided.

Ginger and I kept in touch after she left the treatment center, went through college, and then entered the business world, where she exhibited the positive side of an addictive personality, of someone channeling obsessive energy toward positive goals. Moving to Seattle, she'd risen through the ranks of a computer microchip firm to become its personnel manager and the only woman on its ten-person corporate board.

Quickly becoming aware of the competitiveness and stress experienced by people in the computer industry as well as their tendency to become insulated from the rest of the world (including, sometimes, their own families), Ginger worked hard to establish an employee assistance program. Ultimately she succeeded in convincing the other board members that it made better financial sense to rehabilitate chemical-dependent employees and salvage their training and talent than it did to terminate them. But even though she acquired the other board members' grudging support for her cause, she didn't win their participation. During the three interventions I'd done at her firm, all "employee assistance" was in her hands.

Swinging my chair back around, I turned my attention to the remaining call messages and the stack of "active" folders piled high on my desk. The next time I looked at the clock, it was almost 4:30. I dialed Ginger's number again. Her secretary had to page her, but Ginger came on the line a few moments later. "You've probably already guessed, Ed. I want you to do another intervention. And for this person, the sooner the better."

"Who is it?" I asked.

Ginger gave me a brief history of a young woman named Lorraine Jackson who had been working at Ginger's firm for almost two years. Born in Seattle's "black barrio," Lorraine had been initiated into the drug world when she started sniffing glue in sixth grade. At age thirteen, she was a multiple-drug user; at fifteen a high school dropout; at sixteen an unwed mother. Then she married a drug dealer, who fathered her second child. When he was arrested for possession, Lorraine found herself alone on the street with two small children.

And that, Ginger said, was when the young woman decided to fight back.

Lorraine got herself off drugs, found a welfare-supported nursery to care for her children, enrolled in an extension program to complete her high school diploma, then entered a vocational school, where she discovered she had an aptitude for mastering computer languages. After graduating from the vocational school, Lorraine went to work at Ginger's firm, and for the first time in her nineteen-year-old life, her future looked bright. But little by little, the combined stress of single-parenting and her demanding job began to break her down.

People who have attained abstinence but haven't affiliated with an ongoing recovery program (an anonymous self-help group or one led by a qualified therapist) have to be very careful. Addiction is always lying in wait, and any person who has once connected with a drug carries a recorded psychological message inside that plays back whenever they're stressed or in pain: "You don't have to feel bad—take a drink, pop a pill, shoot up." Even though the payoff can be devastating, the brain says, "It feels good."

One night Lorraine came home from work so exhausted she couldn't stop yelling at her children. To calm her, her live-in baby-sitter offered to "kick her down" on heroin—one of the few drugs Lorraine had never tried.

The "rush" of heroin fades in minutes into the lethargic "nod," which, for beginning users, can last six to twelve hours. It is characterized by feelings of warmth, contentment, and an absence of anxiety—exactly what Lorraine was craving. Lorraine's reaction to the drug was intense. Heroin made all her problems disappear, and she wanted them to stay invisible, permanently.

Ginger said, "A few months ago, the state took Lorraine's kids away from her and put them in foster homes. Now I hear she's holding open house at her apartment every weekend. Anyone who comes has to kick her down. Lately, she's been alternating crystal meth and heroin."

That's one of the most lethal drug combinations there is. To jolt themselves out of their "trance," some heroin users will inject methamphetamine. The inevitable aftermath of the chemical interplay between a narcotic and a stimulant is depression, insomnia, exhaustion, and mental disorganization.

I asked Ginger, "I don't imagine Lorraine's still functioning at work?"

"No. At the staff meeting this afternoon, the other board members voted to fire her. On the basis of her first year's performance, I asked them to grant her a leave of absence to enter a treatment program. They agreed to forty-five days."

"That gets it down to the wire," I said. "What kind of physical shape is she in?"

"Just about what you'd imagine. Undernourished and anemic, close to the edge when she can't make a buy."

"When do you want me to intervene?"

"Before the weekend if you possibly can, Ed. And preferably in the morning. Lorraine has a tendency to disappear after lunch."

I looked at my calendar. "I could make Friday open."

"Friday's fine," Ginger said. "In fact, that's payday, so I know she'll be here."

We talked for a while about treatment centers, and Ginger said she'd make the arrangements.

I told her I'd catch the 7:00 A.M. flight out of Long Beach, rent a car at the airport, and be at her office by 10:30.

After a small beat of silence, Ginger said, "Ed, I can practically guarantee the other board members will all have previous appointments. It's going to be just you and me again."

"So?" I said. "We make a good team."

After we said good-bye, I studied my calendar once more, wishing I could intervene sooner. Alternating crystal meth and heroin is the chemical equivalent of Russian roulette. But Friday was the best I could do. I did expect the intervention itself to go relatively smoothly. Lorraine's job was the one area of her life where she'd experienced success, and the fact that she was still showing up for work made me believe she was trying to hang on to that.

The Friday sunrise was coloring the horizon shades of rose, lavender, and pink as I drove toward the Long Beach Airport. I expected the usual gray drizzle in Seattle, but the skies stayed blue all the way and the sun was shining brilliantly when the plane landed at Jackson Field.

Ginger's firm was headquartered in a ten-story glass-walled office building in the heart of downtown Seattle. When I gave my name to the receptionist, she told me to take the executive express elevator up to the tenth floor; Ms. Nash was expecting me.

Stepping out into the softly lit corridor on the top floor, I saw Ginger. We never know whether to shake hands or hug, so we do both. She said, "Lorraine is in my office. She's pretty ragged—which is usually the case just before payday when she's had to thin out her heroin."

She took me to a conference room, and we went over our strategy. After about fifteen minutes of discussion, I nodded, said, "Let's go talk to her," and we went to Ginger's office. Ginger introduced me to her assistant in the reception area, then we went into the inner room and she closed the door softly.

A used-looking young woman was sitting in a chair near the window, staring out. Her skin was a warm nutmeg color. Her large dark eyes, which should have been beautiful, weren't. The whites had a yellowy tinge that made me wonder if she'd picked up hepatitis from sharing the needle. She had on a long-sleeved blouse, and I suspected all her clothes had long sleeves these days.

I also got the immediate impression that her connection to

the world Ginger and I inhabited was web-thin and it wasn't going to be easy to get through to her.

Her eyes slid slowly from me to Ginger, back to me.

"Lorraine, my name is Ed Storti. I'm a friend of Ginger's. She's asked me to come here and talk to you."

"About what?" she said dully.

"Getting help for your addiction."

"Shit," she murmured. "No way." And she turned back to the window.

"Lorraine!"

Ginger's urgent voice turned the young woman's head toward her.

"Get some help! In your whole life, you've never had any."

"Needle's all the help I need."

"It isn't 'helping' you," Ginger said, "it's killing you."

"Then it's a fine way to go. Gives me this real warm butterfly feeling inside and I just flo-o-at away. 'S what I need to make me happy, 's what I'm always going to hang on to, no matter what."

I said, "Lorraine, Ginger told me what you were like when you came to work here—bright, gutsy, full of pizzazz. I'd like to meet that person."

Lorraine shook her head. "She's long gone."

"Then let's get her back," I said. "You got yourself off drugs once. Do it again—only not alone this time."

"What for?"

"Because right now I'm looking at a young woman in hell who doesn't have to be there."

A slow smile. "Honey, hell is what's 'out there' waiting if I let go of the needle. I'm being evicted, owe people money. I've lost my kids. My job, too, I suppose." The eyes slid over to Ginger. "That what you called me up here to tell me?"

"You've got forty-five days," Ginger said.

"What's that mean?"

"A leave of absence."

Frowning, Lorraine mouthed the words as if she were trying to make sense out of them.

Ginger went on, "We've got a place for you in a good treatment center. You'll have to work harder than you ever have in your life, but you can get better there."

"Nuh-*uh*."

Suddenly Ginger stood up, moved swiftly around her desk to stand next to Lorraine. "I wish I could have your kids brought here right this minute. I'd be sorry to have them see you the way you look now, but it would be better for them to see you here like this than later in your coffin. Which is where you're going to end up if you go back out on the streets. That's some legacy."

Ginger's words hit a nerve, and Lorraine's eyes darted up, raking Ginger's face. Swearing softly, she reached out and grabbed the first thing her fingers touched on Ginger's desk, a brass pencil bucket. The pencils went flying as Lorraine threw it across the room. I started toward her, but Ginger gestured me back and quickly moved other objects on her desk within Lorraine's reach. "Here! Throw these! It makes about as much sense as everything else you're doing with your life."

Lorraine's hand shot up to hit Ginger, but Ginger was too quick for her. She grabbed the other woman's wrists. Lorraine's brief adrenaline flare sputtered out. She huddled into the chair as far back as she could and started to cry.

I said, "Lorraine, Ginger and I know what you're feeling. We've been there."

Lorraine shook her head. "No way you've been as far down as me."

Ginger said, "When you're straight, I'll swap down-and-out stories."

I said, "You can save your life, your sanity, and your job, and get your kids back. Ginger values and respects you. She's a strong lady to have in your corner. And I'll tell you something else, Lorraine—the treatment center sure beats the streets."

She shook her head. "Too tired."

She wasn't just tired, she was spent. I was grateful for her brief flare of temper, because it had depleted her strength to resist.

"Come on, Lorraine," I said. "One step."

Silence.

I held out my hand. "How about as far as the door."

A deep, shuddering sigh.

My fingers touched hers. She didn't pull away. I took hold of her hand, drew her up out of the chair, saw the needle marks marring her twig-thin forearm through the sheer cloth of her blouse. I hadn't realized until we got her on her feet how painfully emaciated the young woman was. With me holding her up on one side, Ginger on the other, we walked out of the office and down the corridor, and inwardly I gave thanks for Ginger and her courage and compassion.

The treatment center was in a suburb north of the city. I drove as fast as Seattle's speed limit allowed, and Ginger held Lorraine's hand all the way. By the time we pulled up to the entrance, the young woman was trembling and drenched in perspiration. A bed was ready for her in detox, and two medical staff members were waiting to take her to it.

Lorraine's detoxification was difficult, and she tried to "walk" the second night, which is fairly typical behavior for a heroin user. The staff called Ginger; Ginger got there quickly, stayed with Lorraine until dawn, and succeeded in talking her down.

Lorraine remained in treatment for forty days, then went to live in a halfway house with ten other women recovering from chemical dependency.

The last time I talked to Ginger, Lorraine had regained custody of her children and was back at work full-time.

In the early part of this century, there may have been as many substance-dependent women in proportion to the population as there are today, but many kept their addiction invisible or called it something else. For example, the family doctor labeled Adele O'Brien's mother's addiction to Dilaudid "neurasthenia," and the periods of time she spent in sanitariums were "rest cures."

Also, addicted women who spent upward of 80 percent of their time in their homes could and often did disguise their disease from friends and neighbors, sometimes even from their own families. But entering the workplace, women vulnerable to addiction were unable to hide it when substance dependency took over their lives.

I intervene with women addicted to alcohol, cocaine, heroin, amphetamines, and Valium and other prescription drugs. But a substantial number of the interventions I do with women are focused on the eating disorders that experts currently estimate affect one out of five women in America. Considering the association of food with the traditional nurturing roles working women today are struggling so hard to reshape and redefine, perhaps that statistic isn't surprising.

Anorexia nervosa, the starvation of the self that disables teenage girls experiencing identity crises and fear of growing up, is estimated to afflict one in two hundred girls between sixteen and eighteen years of age. The "typical" anorexic comes from an achievement-oriented home, is a "model" child from early childhood on, believes she is valued and loved for what she does rather than who she is. During puberty, a time when she is most apt to come in conflict over control issues with her parents, she quickly discovers that eating is one area of her life she *can* control. ·

I find anorexia the most difficult eating disorder to intervene with—partly because anorexic young women are so often addicted to amphetamines at toxic levels, which in itself erodes emotional stability. Also, anorexics defend their right to stay in pain more than any other addictive individuals, more even than the most confirmed alcoholic. And anorexics have a distorted body image that is as impenetrable as a coat of armor. They see themselves as too fat when, in reality, they are painfully, skeletally thin.

Bulimarexia, the disorder that causes women to go on eating binges, then purge themselves by self-induced vomiting or the use of laxatives, affects a large number of college coeds (current estimates range between 10 and 20 percent) as well as young, single, successful professional women, many of whom become preoccupied with suicidal thoughts in the course of their disease. Even so, they are easier to motivate to accept help than anorexics. Their body image is not distorted, and there is no way the binge/purge cycle can be romanticized the way starvation often is by anorexics.

Also responsive to intervention are women who suffer from an obsessive-compulsive eating disorder, which at its extreme is called bulimia and is characterized by binge eating, but without purging. Obsessive-compulsive eaters are at least 20 percent overweight and are unable—no matter how many times they try—to maintain an appropriate weight. They alternate between excessive eating and frequent, futile diets, are haunted by depression and guilt. Many attempt to appease their anxieties by focusing their attention on the "perfect body" and "the diet." These are the women who, in the diet cycle of their addictive disease, pore over calorie charts, weigh chicken breasts down to the quarter ounce, measure waist and ankles and thighs several times a day, trudge grimly along joggers' routes hoping to walk off unwanted pounds. They tend to be cooperative in interventions, because most want so desperately to please the people they're close to. Facing a caring circle of family and friends in an intervention, they will immediately agree to enter treatment. Often, in fact, a full-scale intervention isn't even necessary. A simple home consultation involving one or two family members, with the food-addicted person knowing in advance that I am coming to discuss her or his eating

162

disorder, is all that it takes to motivate the addicted person to enter treatment.

The down side is that obsessive-compulsive overeating is one of the most difficult addictions to put in remission. One reason is the conjuring power of food itself. Detoxification from other substances—alcohol, cocaine, heroin, marijuana, amphetamines—is achieved in treatment by removing access to those substances. Food cannot be removed from the environment, and the act of eating or seeing any food often reinforces the obsessive-compulsive eater's longing for whatever food she is craving.

A second reason compulsive overeating is difficult to put in remission is that at some point during the course of their obsession with food, overweight people learn not to respond to the jibes and jokes and worse forms of cruelty this world metes out to them. But in the cocoonlike environment of treatment, all that anger, resentment, and despair they have submerged for years comes out.

And finally, compulsive overeaters have the same palette of personality traits other addictive people do. To camouflage their excruciatingly poor addictive self-images, many enhance, even overenhance, their positive traits. Most compulsive overeaters I have worked with are extremely good-hearted and generous people who try to "be there" for their family and friends, no matter the cost to their own lives. They demand perfection from themselves in whatever domestic or work situation they're engaged in, and are happiest when in complete control of their nonfood environment. In treatment, they miss these compensatory life patterns they've worked so hard to establish, and become, for a while, very angry people.

Like Miriam Jenkins.

Miriam

Miriam was a nurse in the OB-GYN unit in a midsize suburban hospital in Phoenix, Arizona.

Like most compulsive eaters, Miriam became fascinated with food at an early age. This may have been intensified by the fact that she was born in England shortly before World War II and grew up in a time of food rationing and deprivation. Also, she had nine brothers and sisters. At best, food was never plentiful in Miriam's household, and both her parents worked to make ends meet. Miriam's mother was a "charwoman" for wealthy families, and before Miriam reached school age she would often take the child to work with her. Miriam remembers being infatuated by the rich array of food in wealthy people's cupboards and gradually coming to equate "the good life" with such abundance.

Sweets were difficult, sometimes impossible, to get during those years of rationing, and an often-used substitute was slices of bread spread thickly with butter and condensed milk. Miriam remembers craving the condensed-milk sandwiches whenever she was unhappy, and ultimately skipping the bread to eat the condensed milk right out of the can. When she was hospitalized for a painful mastoid condition, her entire family—parents, brothers and sisters, aunts, uncles, and cousins—hoarded their ration tickets to obtain what they knew would be the greatest treat imaginable for Miriam: ice cream. Doing so, they also, unwittingly, reinforced her growing belief in food as a pain reliever.

By the time she left home in the late 1950s to enter nursing school, Miriam was unconsciously using food as an emotional pacifier. A rule existed in England then that young women engaged to marry could not be nursing students. Miriam, however, was secretly engaged, and when an administrator at the school found out, Miriam was expelled. Her immediate reaction to the crushing of her career hopes was to eat. Within two months, she had gained forty pounds and the compulsive eating pattern that would characterize her eating disorder for years to come was established: when unhappy, she would eat little during the day, then gorge herself at night.

Miriam and her husband, Joe, emigrated to the United States in the early 1960s. Miriam completed her nurse's training in Arizona and had no trouble finding a job. She was a good nurse, empathic with her patients; she got along well with her peers and derived satisfaction from her work. At the same time, she suffered acute bouts of homesickness. She also often allowed herself to be intimidated or "put down" by doctors—telling herself that was a result of having grown up as a "less than" in England's class system.

Joe worked nights, so Miriam had the house—and kitchen—to herself. Whenever she had a bad day at work, she would come home filled with that sense of void so many obsessive eaters talk about, that feeling there isn't enough food in the world to fill the emptiness inside. Many evenings, Miriam would start out promising herself she was just going to have one bowl of ice cream, then become fixated on having the level of the ice cream perfectly even within its half-gallon container. She would "trim the edges" with her spoon until she hit bottom. Other evenings she craved fried foods. She would fry the obvious first—potatoes and meat and eggs— then move on to foods even people with "stir-fry mania" wouldn't think of frying—cucumbers, peanuts, cottage cheese.

For almost two decades, Miriam (like women in earlier eras) kept her addiction as "unseen" as possible. Not secret. She knew everyone close to her was aware of her compulsive eating. But she tried not to eat excessively in front of others.

The most difficult food-related times for her at work occurred when grateful patients gifted the nursing staff with boxes of chocolates. The candy boxes would be placed, open, on the countertop at the nursing station so that staff members could help themselves when they felt like it. Miriam would wait for moments when the corridor was deserted, then lift up the top layer and take chocolates from the "unseen" bottom layer.

About once every six months, she channeled the driving

energy of her food obsession into dieting and starved herself compulsively on lettuce and grapefruit or whatever fare the diet allowed. But, as she put it, "my cravings would surface like the Loch Ness Monster," and she fell off each diet, giving her food addiction what it wanted.

These swings between dieting and gluttony wreaked havoc on her endocrine system as well as her disposition. Although she tried and for the most part succeeded in concealing her self-rage at work, sometimes it flared; she would explode at discovering towels stacked crookedly in a supply closet or the sound of a squeaky wheelchair.

She was terrified when Joe was transferred from night to day shift and she no longer had the kitchen to herself, until she discovered she really didn't care whether Joe saw her eat excessively or not—a point most obsessive/compulsive eaters reach.

Inevitably, her health was endangered. Some days, despite her overwhelming sense of duty toward her job and patients, she was in such acute abdominal distress that she could neither sit nor lie down, let alone go to work. Her coworkers and supervisor, aware of the quickening downward spiral of her disease, decided to intervene.

Joe, having sat beside Miriam evening after evening in front of the TV, watching her eat and eat and pay no attention to his criticism or disapproval or concern, believed it would be futile for him to participate, though he didn't oppose the hospital staff's intervening.

When Miriam's nursing supervisor contacted me, I was optimistic about the outcome of intervening with Miriam. I believed she, like over 90 percent of the obsessive overeaters I'd worked with, would be easy to motivate into treatment.

As it turned out, something happened that took me completely by surprise. Even though I've grown used to coping with the unexpected—key participants failing to show up, the people I'm intervening with running away (and sometimes coming back!)—what happened with Miriam had never happened before, and hasn't since.

I agreed to fly to Phoenix to meet with her supervisor and coworkers at the hospital on one of Miriam's days off. The plan was: (1) to prepare the staff; (2) to help the hospital's employee assistance administrator choose an appropriate treatment center in or near Phoenix before I flew home; (3) then return to Phoenix to lead the intervention when admission arrangements were complete—which I judged would take about a week.

Everything started out smoothly. I flew to Phoenix, drove to the hospital, met briefly with Miriam's supervisor in a small conference room adjacent to the nurses' station. Then the nurses and staff members who were going to participate in the intervention entered the room and took seats among the circle of chairs I'd arranged. I introduced myself, talked to them about obsessive-compulsive eating as an addictive disease, and was just beginning to explore each of their relationships with Miriam to determine who my prime motivators might be during the intervention when the door to the conference room opened and a woman I knew had to be Miriam stood staring in at us with frightened, angry eyes. She was short and small-boned, and her delicate wrists and ankles were buried in rolls of fat. Her normally pale complexion was suffused with a hot mottled pink as her eyes tallied the faces of her administrator and coworkers, who sat staring back at her in stunned silence.

I moved toward her quickly, holding out my hand, telling her my name and what I was there for. With a spontaneity I was immensely grateful for, Miriam's supervisor and coworkers rose and moved close to her, several embracing her, all of them speaking of their deep concern for her well-being.

The hot color slowly ebbed from Miriam's cheeks as her fear and sense of betrayal were allayed by the expressions of compassion she was hearing. When I saw her respond to one woman by hugging her back, I believed I could successfully intervene then and there.

Miriam murmured that she had come in to do some catch-up work on her nursing charts. Since the chart rack was right next to the conference-room door, she couldn't help overhearing what was being said.

I invited her to sit next to me in the circle of chairs and motioned to Miriam's close friend (the woman she'd hugged) to sit on the other side.

I told Miriam she had taken us by surprise at least as much as we had her. I asked if she had overheard one word spoken by anyone in that room that had not been filled with caring and concern for her well-being.

She acknowledged she had not.

I said I hoped the end result of this meeting would be that she would enter treatment even sooner than she might have otherwise. I spoke to Miriam for about ten minutes on the disease of addiction, to allow the group time to grow calm and collect their thoughts. I purposefully stayed soft and gentle, hoping the participants would mirror that attitude. Then I asked each person in the room to express her or his feelings about Miriam's addiction and its destructiveness to her health and work. The last person I called on was Miriam's friend sitting next to her, and at the end of her friend's deeply caring statement, Miriam agreed to enter treatment.

But even as I moved toward closing, a question loomed large in my mind. Where was I going to put her? No admittance arrangements had even been begun.

I asked Miriam's supervisor and friend to remain with her while I went to talk to the hospital's employee assistance administrator. I was two hours early for our scheduled appointment, but he was able to see me immediately.

To our dismay, we discovered none of the high-quality centers in Phoenix that treated eating disorders would be able to admit Miriam for three days.

I had never led an intervention where admission arrangements hadn't been confirmed in advance, and I honestly didn't know what the outcome of waiting would be for Miriam. The grimmest possibility I could envision was that she would go on an eating binge that would do her physical harm; the second, that she would quit her job, get another one at another hospital, and continue surrendering her life to her addictive disease.

I went back into the room with the administrator, presented the treatment plan to Miriam, and got what seemed to me a firm promise she would enter treatment in three days.

The way Miriam spent those days confirmed the perfectionism and desire to please that is so characteristic of the compulsive eater. At the hospital, she dotted every *i* and crossed every *t* on her medical charts and made certain the nurses who would be working her shift hours understood the needs and idiosyncrasies of her patients. At home, she washed her windows, polished her floors, and saw to it the refrigerator and cupboard were well stocked for Joe. On day three, Joe accompanied her to the center.

Miriam had a difficult time in treatment. Her obsessive-compulsive eating had gone unchecked for three decades. Her physical health had to be stabilized by the medical staff before eating-disorders counselors could begin working with her to help her change her ideas about her self-image, nutrition, and food. Predictably, it was far easier to stabilize Miriam physically than it was emotionally.

Though she had gained a great deal of insight into her addictive disease by the time she left the treatment center, Miriam firmly believes that had it not been for her participation in OA (Overeaters Anonymous), forged during treatment, she would not be in remission today.

In an OA group, attaining abstinence requires giving up the foods one is most obsessed by—which for Miriam were ice cream and fried foods.

Self-sabotage exists in all addictions, and it's especially

seductive in food addiction. Even though Miriam recognized the beginning symptoms of relapse with acute clarity—making excuses to stay home alone, not answering the telephone, refusing to talk with her OA sponsor, missing her OA meetings—she nevertheless suffered three relapses. Yet each time, she resumed her fight against her addiction with renewed determination, and the last time I spoke with her she had been abstinent from her "self-destructive foods" for more than a year.

It isn't always a supervisor and/or peers who initiate an intervention. Sometimes it's a subordinate.

Rosemary and Monte

Monte was a college president. Rosemary, his secretary, had been his enabler for years—smoothing over appointments he missed, handling his personal and professional correspondence, arranging for other faculty members to make public appearances when he couldn't.

One Monday morning Monte fell in his office, hitting his head on the corner of his desk. It was a nasty wound that required several stitches, and it made Rosemary realize her attempts to "help" could actually be imperiling her boss's life.

Because of all the covering up she'd done, she was convinced no one knew about the severity of Monte's drinking problem, and so she anticipated skepticism when she asked the vice-chancellor and two senior faculty members to participate in an intervention. To her surprise, they expressed their utter relief that someone at last was taking action. They promised their wholehearted cooperation.

By then, Monte was in the habit of holding sensitive meetings involving college matters in a restaurant/bar near campus. The vice-chancellor stated that "when Monte set up a round, he wanted everyone to partake. That didn't augur well for the college's reputation, or ours. I told Monte that once, and he gave me a strange look that said 'I know' but at the time, he was telling me in words, 'Don't be such a worryhound. You take things too seriously.' "

Monte's intervention was one of the shortest I've ever led. The morning Rosemary led us into Monte's office, I barely had time to tell him what I was there for before Monte said, "Let's go." He stated he'd known for a long time he was an alcoholic, but he just didn't know what to do about it.

He did spectacularly well in treatment. The fact that nobody had ever confronted him about his drinking had convinced him his associates and friends believed he was beyond help. He said his predominant emotion the morning Rosemary, his colleagues, and I entered his office was a sense of deliverance.

———

Of course, there are always the tough cases that balance out the easy ones. And sometimes even when a person's job is on the line, I can't get through. It certainly can happen when the person's drug of choice is marijuana.

It surprises many people when I say that. Yet I believe marijuana may be the least-understood drug used today. Excessive use of heroin or cocaine or alcohol generates physical and mental deterioration that eventually becomes so obvious that it demands attention. But marijuana's effects are far more cryptic. And I, personally, have seen so much blighted ambition and apathy associated with heavy use of this drug, I never think of or treat it lightly.

Brian

I once intervened with a thirty-four-year-old man, Brian, who had been using marijuana heavily for twenty years. He was employed by his father in a construction firm. Knowing from the father's description of his son's behavior that I would need as much leverage as I could get, I asked the father if he would be willing to tell Brian he couldn't return to work until he'd undergone treatment. The father agreed.

However, the man's wife resisted when I suggested she

take her children and leave if her husband refused to enter treatment. I know the idea of marriage often symbolizes safety and security long after a spouse's behavior has destroyed both—as this man's certainly had (he was frequently verbally abusive and sometimes physically). I wanted this woman and her children to have a chance at improving their lives. I could also tell that her parents, sister, and in-laws would support and help if she did leave. And we finally persuaded her to take the children and stay with her sister if it became necessary.

During the intervention, Brian listened passively while his parents, wife, relatives, coworkers, and even his young sons told him how his life was being ruined by marijuana. He didn't get angry or sad—he scarcely reacted at all. It was as if he were peering out through a murky fog, could see and hear, but everything was dulled by the time it reached him.

At the end he simply said, "You all do what you have to. I'm going to smoke some joints and watch the Angels game."

He'd been fourteen when he became psychologically dependent on marijuana. His behavior confirmed my belief that when adolescents use drugs or liquor to avoid their problems, they remain adolescent, emotionally, until they stop using, because working through problems is part of the maturation process. If you don't work, you don't grow. Brian was chronologically thirty-four but twenty years younger in every other way.

The father and wife kept their commitments. The wife took the children and went to stay with her sister. The father told his son not to come to work on Monday.

Brian did enter treatment after the World Series was over, but sabotaged his recovery by walking off the grounds during recreation and smoking a joint. The staff ordered a drug test, which came out positive, and he was clinically discharged.

Brian was not given his job back. His wife entered therapy,

joined a self-help group, eventually divorced Brian and remarried.

Marijuana's enervating behavioral effects become much more observable among heavy users of hashish, a concentrated resin made from cannabis leaves and flowers and hashish oil (an alcoholic extract of cannabis). More concentrated than marijuana, it's also observably physically damaging. Heavy smoking of hashish reduces lung capacity; it results in shortness of breath and finally chronic bronchitis. That deep, scarifying cough was certainly observable in Yousef in one of the most mystifying and exhausting workplace-initiated interventions I've ever done.

Yousef

My first contact on Yousef's case was with an ex-policeman who told me his name was George Jordan. I have no idea whether that was his real name or whether anyone involved in this case gave me a real name.

During our first face-to-face meeting in my office, George told me he had left the police force in a large midwestern city to become West Coast public affairs representative in charge of security and business arrangements for the members of a wealthy Arabian cartel that had offices in Beverly Hills, New York, Paris, London, Rome, and the city of Jeddah in Saudi Arabia.

George said the head of the cartel had gotten my name from a well-known treatment center in Beverly Hills. The members of the cartel wanted me to intervene with Yousef, a forty-year-old multimillionaire whose addiction to hashish and alcohol was imparing his ability to function productively.

I assumed that since George had driven to my office from Beverly Hills, that was where the intervention would take place.

George said no; although arrangements had been made to admit Yousef to the treatment center there, they wanted me to fly to Jeddah to do the intervention.

"How soon?" I asked.

"A week."

I was positive it would take at least a month to obtain a visa and renew my passport.

George said those matters could be expedited, and they were. A few days later I had my passport and visa in hand, and exactly one week after my conversation with George, I was on a plane for Paris, the first stop on my journey to Jeddah.

I was met at De Gaulle Airport by two Arabians dressed in Western business suits who spoke impeccable English and French. They drove me to a flat on Avenue Foch, where I was served dinner in the evening and breakfast on rising, after which the two men drove me to the airport to catch my flight to Jeddah.

The flight was long and hot and crowded. I was already suffering from jet lag and a throbbing headache—unusual for me, because normally I don't get headaches.

When I stepped out of the air bus, the heat off the desert came at me in a great blast, and so did culture shock. I saw Arabian men in thin flowing robes, veiled women in long capes, and army officers in white tunics carrying rifles.

Again I was greeted by two men in Western business suits, who informed me courteously that if I had pornographic magazines or alcoholic beverages in my suitcase, they would not pass through customs. (In his "briefing," George had told me that Islam forbids drinking alcohol, and alcohol is not permitted in Saudi Arabia. King Ibn Saud had at one time allowed the diplomatic corps in Arabia to have liquor for their own use, but that privilege was rescinded by the king when one of his subjects, already drunk, burst in on the British consul demanding liquor from the consulate's private stock. The consul refused, and the intoxicated Arab became so incensed that he shot and killed the Englishman. After that unfortunate incident, those who wanted alcoholic beverages had to either smuggle them in or make them themselves.)

I assured my escorts that I had no alcohol or magazines.

They said they would drop my bags off at my hotel, then take me to meet Yousef's wife, sister, brother-in-law, and widowed mother. Although the intervention had been arranged by members of the cartel, it was in keeping with Arabian custom that it take place within the family.

I desperately wanted an aspirin, a bath, and a nap—in that order. My dismay must have shown on my face, because one of my escorts said simply, "You are expected," and I understood it would do no good to argue. They were simply doing with me what they had been told.

I was driven in a Rolls-Royce to an ornate rambling structure which, I soon learned, housed Yousef's sister and her husband and family and Yousef's mother in lavish separate apartment suites on the upper story, while the ground-floor apartments were given over to the conducting of business.

I followed a servant up a plushly carpeted stairway to the second story, then down a corridor of murals into a living room, where I was introduced to Yousef's family members. Then I was invited to sit on a damask-covered couch and partake of tea from a gleaming silver tea service.

I was exhausted and felt grimy and disheveled from my journey. In contrast, Yousef's family—his mother, wife, sister, brother-in-law—were beautifully garbed and groomed. They had been eagerly awaiting my arrival and were anxious to begin.

As I wearily started the preparation, I quickly became cognizant of two things that were certainly going to affect the outcome of this intervention: Yousef's brother-in-law had a drug problem of his own and was not going to be a reliable participant; and the women, though they were as charming and gracious as they could be, were relying on the brother-in-law to carry the intervention, because their culture required them to be passive.

I think it was a combination of my exhaustion and my

conviction that I could not carry an intervention on my own in a culture that was alien to me—as I would have done or attempted to do in America—that made me cut through the amenities.

I told them I had to have a powerful person at the intervention, someone Yousef would listen to. I asked whether such a person was available.

They were all unhappy with my question. Yousef's wife said that even though the intervention had been arranged by the cartel, they wished to carry it out within the family.

I said I doubted Yousef would accede to his family's wishes, especially since the women were unable to make strong statements.

The brother-in-law finally said one of the senior cartel members, Shayek Rashid, was in Jeddah but it would take time to arrange a meeting with him.

Translating "time" in an American way, I believed he meant a day, or at the most two, to set up a meeting with Shayek Rashid. I said I would wait.

But one day passed into another, into another.

I began to feel a little like a captive, because my passport and visa had been taken by the men who met me at the airport. At the end of the week, the brother-in-law left for Paris, and I was told he might not be back for a month. I didn't think his absence would affect the outcome of the intervention very much; Shayek Rashid was the one whose presence was going to be important. But my inquiries each morning and afternoon as to when the meeting would take place were met with the same courteous reply: "When Rashid is not busy, he will see you."

The waiting was difficult for me. Jeddah is a beautiful city, but you don't just go wandering out into the sand dunes in Arabia to pass the time—which hung heavily, even though the women did their best to entertain me. Riding veiled and in separate cars from the one that was put at my disposal, they took me to the gold markets and the rug markets, had lavish luncheons prepared in their apartments, even invited me to attend the beheading of a rapist one day (I declined). Their words when we parted each evening—*Tisbahi-ala-khar,* "May you waken in goodness, good night"—were utterly sincere. The hours I spent with them taught me that hospitality is a source of pride with Arabs, and although the gestures, the speech, the actions conform to patterns long established, there is nothing false in them. An atmosphere of genuine welcome is imparted, and I always had the feeling I was an honored guest.

Yet despite their kindness, I grew more and more homesick and anxious to bring my mission to an end. At last I was informed Shayek Rashid would give me five minutes. On the appointed afternoon, he sent his limousine to my hotel.

He was a tall, elegant, impressive man. The moment I made eye contact with him, I knew he would exude strength. I explained the intervention process, stressed the importance of a "power person," and said I needed his presence.

Rashid said, "Of course. If it is agreeable to you, my wife will call Yousef's wife and tell her we are coming to dinner this evening and we will bring this matter to a conclusion."

Inwardly, I uttered, *Alhamdulilah*—"Thanks be to the Almighty."

I was driven back to the hotel, and, alone in my room, went over my case for the hundredth time. I had been told in some detail how serious Yousef's condition was. In addition to being heavily into hashish, he drank excessively on his trips out of Arabia and had an enlarged liver, anemia, and chronic pancreatitis. It was imperative that he receive medical treatment, and I hoped for the sake of his mental and physical health he would attain and remain in sobriety.

The limousine came for me again that evening, and I rode with Rashid to Yousef's house while Rashid's wife rode in another limousine behind ours.

As we drew up to Yousef's home—a newly built, palatial residence overlooking the Red Sea coast in the northeast sector of Jeddah—I saw my patient for the first time. I could tell he had once been handsome, but his illness was revealed in his pale, almost translucent skin, and in the weariness in his face. He came to our car, greeted Rashid by kissing his left cheek, his right cheek, and then his nose. Then he looked at me.

I said, "My name is Ed. Who I am will be explained to you."

And he said, "Of course, of course."

By then I thought I had become immune to opulence. But the carved ceilings, rococo furniture, and oriental carpets in Yousef's home filled me with awe.

We were served the mandatory elegant tea in the parlor, and then I opened up the intervention. Because I was restricted from talking about alcohol and it would have been discourteous to mention hashish, I used the term "chemical dependency" throughout. I told Yousef that because of the grave state of his health, he needed to enter a treatment center immediately, and that arrangements had been made for him in Beverly Hills.

Tears immediately came to his eyes. I could tell that Rashid's presence made him both frightened and ashamed. I felt compassion for him. And yet I sensed that alone with me and the three women, he would have been immovably resistant.

Even with Rashid there, he said, "I cannot go. I have too many business interests to watch over."

I asked the women to express their concerns, and they did, his wife saying movingly, "You mean everything to me, and this man will take you away and you will get help."

Then something happened that took me totally by surprise. The women started to speak to Yousef, and he to them, in Arabic. I watched the conversation like a tennis match. I had no idea what they were saying, but since I had become aware during my stay in Jeddah what a bartering nation the Arabs were, I thought Yousef might be bargaining for time, and knowing the passive position the women were required to take, I was afraid he might succeed.

At the first interval I was able to get a word in, I turned to Rashid and said, "Do you believe Yousef should get help immediately?"

Rashid said quietly, "Yousef, you will go with this man."

I could tell from the texture of the immediate silence that Rashid's statement was the whole intervention.

Yousef bowed his head and replied, "Of course."

And that was it. Or almost.

For Yousef and me, and perhaps everyone, the most difficult part of the evening lay ahead. Custom and courtesy demanded we eat the dinner Yousef's wife had had prepared for us—food enough for twenty-five people served on golden plates, with a servant attending upon each diner.

Yousef's distress was obvious. I didn't see how anyone could have any appetite. I certainly didn't. But the dinner had to be gotten through, and get through it we did.

The next afternoon, Yousef and I boarded a jet for Paris. We spent the night in opposite wings in the elegant flat on Avenue Foch, and in the morning it was obvious how Yousef had passed the time. We were driven to the airport, boarded Air France, and arrived at the treatment center in Beverly Hills at 10:00 at night.

I had been away from home for a little more than two weeks. It seemed like much longer.

I kept in touch with the people in Jeddah over the next few weeks, relaying Yousef's progress.

He was an extremely difficult patient—imperious and aloof, interacting little with the other patients and thereby depriving himself of one of the greatest gifts treatment has to offer: empathic communication with others who are going through the same thing you are.

Yousef completed the full course of treatment, but six

months after his release, I was not able to find out anything about his whereabouts or his condition.

In retrospect, Yousef's case confirmed to me that it truly doesn't matter whether you are a longshoreman on the docks at San Pedro, an elderly lady alone in a room in a retirement residence in Boston, the wife of the President of the United States in the White House, a well-known comedian at the peak of success in Hollywood, or an Arabian millionaire living in a palatial home on the Red Sea—the effects of addiction are going to be the same. And unless someone—be it family member, friend, neighbor, coworker, or business associate—acts against it, the disease of addiction will ultimately be fatal.

Appendixes

Appendix A: Interventionists

CHOOSING AN INTERVENTIONIST

Many interventionists are on staff at hospitals, treatment centers, or organizations such as the National Council on Alcoholism. In addition to serving as interventionists in these clinical settings, they often act as public outreach coordinators and/or addictive-disease counselors. Most are highly trained, competent individuals.

There are also capable counselors in high schools who act as interventionists with teenagers.

Marriage and family therapists maintain lists of qualified interventionists and will, when asked, make referrals. Some family therapists do interventions themselves.

A small number of interventionists have their own offices and function independently. Among those are nontraditional interventionists willing to intervene in nonclinical settings.

To reach an interventionist, call a reputable hospital or treatment center (several are listed in Appendix D at the end of the book), or an organization such as the National Council on Alcoholism.

The best referral will be from someone who has actually participated in an intervention and has come away with positive feelings about its outcome. Always remember that you are the one who chooses the intervention specialist, so you might talk to a few!

WHAT QUALIFICATIONS SHOULD AN INTERVENTIONIST HAVE?

Some interventionists hold undergraduate and/or graduate degrees in psychology or sociology.

Some are certified alcoholism/drug counselors or marriage and family therapists.

Many are recovering alcoholics or are recovering from addiction to some other substance—cocaine, heroin, food.

Their zeal to help others often derives from their own experience with addiction. But do not choose an interventionist on the basis of whether or not he or she is in recovery from an addiction. Feeling confident and comfortable with the person you choose to represent you is by far the most important factor.

To confirm an interventionist's qualifications, it's certainly appropriate to ask for names and phone numbers of former clients. People who have participated in interventions—relatives, colleagues, and friends of clients—will also act as referral sources.

Yet choosing an interventionist is much like choosing a physician or an attorney. People seeking professional help will usually find an appropriate way to assess that person's qualifications before initiating contact.

HOW IMPORTANT IS A TRACK RECORD?

I often answer this with an analogy. Because I do a lot of commuter flying, I've asked transcontinental airline pilots their opinion of commuter pilots who are just starting out and don't have a lot of air time.

Seasoned pilots reply, "They're fine as long as there's never a problem with the aircraft." In other words, if there should be an emergency, could they respond quickly and solve the problem?

The same thing applies to interventionists. A track record and experience in solving unexpected problems are certainly important. But enthusiasm, courage, the desire to help, and a willingness to learn can and will carry beginners through many difficult situations.

INTERVENTIONISTS' FEES

Hospitals and treatment centers will sometimes arrange for interventionists on their staffs to do clinical interventions for patients who are going to enter treatment. They consider the intervention part of the cost of treatment.

However, an increasing number of facilities are beginning to charge by the hour for time their staff interventionists devote to interventions.

Independent interventionists charge fees for service, and part of their service is helping the family find the most appropriate treatment center for the addicted person.

As in any other profession, the more experienced individuals are and the broader their referral base, the higher their fee. Some charge on an hourly basis, ranging from $100 to $250 per hour. Others charge a fee for the entire process, which ranges from $250 up to and over $1,000. And some operate on a sliding scale based on the person's ability to pay. When the need for intervention is especially urgent, flexible payments usually can be arranged.

TRADITIONAL VERSUS NONTRADITIONAL INTERVENTIONISTS

Traditional clinical interventionists do interventions based on a model Dr. Vernon Johnson originated in the 1960s while working with alcoholism. The primary goal of the Johnson model is to penetrate the alcoholic's denial system by educating and involving family members to help the alcoholic admit his or her drinking problem and get designated assistance.

To accomplish this, traditional interventionists conduct several group meetings with family members, friends, and coworkers, usually in hospital or treatment-center settings. During these meetings, the interventionist endeavors to activate group process among participants—first by educating the members of the group about the disease of addiction, then by guiding them through written assignments to help them find appropriate ways of expressing their feelings to their addicted loved ones. These assignments culminate in letters to be read aloud to the addicted person during a meeting held at the treatment center, hospital, or counseling office, or a neutral home site (rarely at the addicted person's home). The interventionist could be present at the meeting, but would take a fairly passive role. The active role is taken by the participants as they read their letters and present factual data in an effort to persuade the patient to get help. Such a method is intended to fracture the patient's denial so reality can penetrate.

The total time involved—ten to twelve hours of group

meetings, plus one to three hours for the intervention—is usually spread over a period averaging three to four weeks.

I explored Dr. Johnson's model in depth when I was working in a hospital treatment center. I found that most families willing to initiate such traditional interventions were already so determined to act, they were in therapy or participating in an outpatient program, and whether or not the addicted person went into treatment, they would continue to pursue help for themselves.

For the most part, those who rejected the Johnson model did so because they felt it was too time-consuming or the situation they were involved in was too volatile or the number of people able and willing to participate was too small. Often when I told spouses of addicted people I needed more participants from among their wider circle of relatives or friends, they would say no one else was willing to take part.

Increasingly, I found I was only able to use the traditional Johnson model in situations where:

- a group of caring people could be gathered who were able to attend the educational sessions, do the written assignments, and maintain a positive attitude throughout.

- the chemical-dependent person could be motivated to go to a facility or neutral setting where the group intervention meeting was to be held. Or the family could do their own intervention in their own home, with a family member acting as spokesperson.

- there was no imminent crisis, and therefore immediate intervention with the addicted person wasn't necessary.

I wasn't able to use the Johnson model when:

- potentially vital participants were unwilling or unable to take time away from their families and jobs to attend the educational sessions.

- the chemical-dependent person refused to go to the treatment center, hospital, or counselor's office.

- an imminent crisis demanded immediate action.

After I left the hospital setting, I began developing my own nontraditional intervention model that would be responsive to public need, and I made these discoveries:

- I was best able to alleviate the pain of addiction crises by responding to calls for help with a formula permitting instant action when necessary, using a model that could be personalized for each case.

- Participants were far more willing to gather in someone's living room for a single, concentrated preparatory meeting than they were to attend several classes in a clinical setting. They were also able to sustain a more positive attitude during this shorter time span.

- Potentially vital people lost to traditional interventions because their work schedules and personal responsibilities wouldn't allow them to commit the time were, under the flexibility and immediacy of the nontraditional model, able and willing to participate.

- I could, under special and critical circumstances, prepare people by phone who wouldn't otherwise have attended the intervention because circumstances prevented them from coming to the preparation meeting.

- Motivational techniques were as important as clinical skills. My clinical skills remained invaluable in helping me "read" people, but motivational skills were equally invaluable in helping maintain positive, goal-directed attitudes among participants and in persuading the addicted person to enter treatment through continuous motivational statements.

- In many interventions, it wasn't denial that prevented the addicted person from getting help; most people freely acknowledged they had a problem with alcohol and/or drugs or food. Instead, it was the human tendency to say "I don't want to think about that today, I'll think about it tomorrow" that prevented them from taking action. The tendency to procrastinate exists in all human beings, but is heightened in addictive individuals. Faced with a unified group of caring loved ones insisting they act *now*, they did.

- Most families were relieved of stress and fear by having the interventionist take charge and assume leadership in guiding participants in what to say and do. Even more fear and anxiety were alleviated when they understood that the interventionist would be a dominant force in the preparation and intervention.

- The unexpected appearance of a group of unified and caring people in the addicted person's home was a far more

187

motivating "jolt" than the reading of prepared data in a clinical or neutral setting.

- My own energy, because it was concentrated within a shorter time span, remained at a higher level, and so did that of the participants. When I first started leading non-traditional interventions, I would often let a day go by between the preparation meeting and the intervention. Now I like to prepare in the evening and intervene the next morning, or prepare in the morning and intervene in the afternoon of the same day. I've learned the less time that elapses between the preparation and the intervention, the more smoothly the intervention will go.

- Because so many people who need an intervention need one immediately, it was vitally important to be able and willing to intervene on holidays and weekends as well as weekdays, and to stay flexible enough to meet the needs of each case.

In summary, I believe both traditional/clinical and nontraditional models of intervention are effective and can offer hope to chemical-dependent people and their families. I also feel it's important to acknowledge that intervention in the broad sense of the word has always taken place whenever human beings offer compassionate, understanding solutions to each other's problems. It has existed for centuries and I trust and believe it always will.

QUALITIES TO LOOK FOR IN AN INTERVENTIONIST

When I'm lecturing on intervention, people frequently ask, "What qualities would *you* look for if you were choosing an interventionist to perform an intervention on a member of your family?" So I've tried to isolate the qualities I feel are crucial. I know all the ones I list below aren't going to be achievable by any single human being. Some aren't going to be easily observable. But people seeking an interventionist can endeavor to affirm them through referral sources.

A CENTERED, BALANCED PERSONAL LIFE

This is essential if the interventionist is going to be able to expend the time and emotional energy it takes to connect with and help people in acute pain. Helping professionals can't give of themselves unless their own lives are in order. This might be difficult to confirm, but it usually goes hand in hand with an interventionist's having an excellent reputation and a broad referral base.

SELF-ESTEEM

Addicted people will sometimes vent their terror and pain on the interventionist because he or she is the person advocating action and change—two things addicted people (and often their family members) fear and resist. So the interventionist must be able to remain unaffected by verbal abuse and know how to turn negative into positive energy. Previous clients and intervention participants can often attest whether or not an interventionist has this ability.

EMOTIONAL INTUITIVENESS

This quality should be discernible in the first contact made with an interventionist. The interventionist must be gentle and compassionate yet able to balance those qualities with firm direction when necessary.

The normal screening of emotions often vanishes during addiction crises. Therefore the interventionist will become a temporarily intimate member of a family group, and it should be apparent he or she views that opportunity as both a challenge and a privilege.

Interventionists must know how to allow individuals being intervened with the opportunity to retain dignity—even if they refuse to enter treatment—by projecting courtesy, empathy, and a sense of dignity from within themselves.

PROFESSIONALISM

The interventionist should be professional in dress, grooming, speech, and manner.

The physical environment of the setting where the client is received should be appropriate and reassuring.

Any interventionist who is in recovery must represent the

most positive aspects of recovery—physically, psychologically, and spiritually.

MOTIVATIONAL SKILLS

Confidence and credibility can be communicated on the phone through tone of voice and information given, and in person through a facial expression or the quality of a handshake.

Through motivational skills, an interventionist should be able to convince even resistant participants to take part in an intervention by intuiting where the fine line is between persuasion and alienation, and when to step forward and when to step back.

Observing the interventionist accomplish this in the pre-preparation and preparation sessions prior to the actual intervention should go a long way toward confirming his or her motivational abilities.

FLEXIBILITY

As the intervention process unfolds, it should become apparent to family members that the interventionist has the flexibility to switch from motivator to clinician to chemical-dependency counselor.

OBJECTIVITY

Family members should experience growing confidence in the interventionist's ability to determine which participants to call on at crucial moments during an intervention.

COMMITMENT

The family should sense the interventionist's passionate commitment to working with people in crisis. That passion is what enables the interventionist to hear and respond to people in pain, prevent catastrophe, and render help.

QUESTIONS TO ASK AN INTERVENTIONIST

How long have you been intervening?

How many interventions have you done?

What percentage of your clients go immediately into treatment?

Many interventionists will quote the standard rate of success— 80 or 90 percent. Ask what their *individual* rate is in motivating patients into treatment.

Can you admit to a treatment facility other than the one where you are on staff?

Some staff interventionists do have the flexibility to admit to a variety of treatment facilities.

Will you provide names and phone numbers of clients you have worked with in recent months?

Any competent interventionist should be willing and able to do this—obviously with prior approval from his or her past clients.

Do you counsel the patient after the patient is in treatment?

Although interventionists monitor patient progress, most "release" the patient to treatment center counselors so they are emotionally free to move on to their next intervention.

Will you intervene more than once if a patient doesn't go into treatment?

Once a comprehensive intervention has been completed, there is no point in duplicating it. A consultation might be appropriate, but not a full intervention.

Are you yourself recovering from an addictive disease?

Be cautious about an interventionist who can only talk about his or her disease and whose knowledge seems limited to that.

If the patient physically bolts or gets verbally abusive, what will you do?

An interventionist should be able to tell you how far he or she normally will go in this process, what's feasible from his or her point of view and what is not.

Do you take a hard or a soft approach?

It's advantageous to have an interventionist who can adapt to whatever is needed in a given situation.

If certain family members or friends are reluctant to participate in an intervention, what can be done?

An interventionist should be able to guide you in ways to motivate family members, friends, and colleagues to attend a preparation meeting, at which point the task of motivation becomes the interventionist's.

What usually happens when you enter an addicted person's home and begin to intervene?

Interventionists should be able to give you both norms and extremes of what they have experienced. What usually happens is that the patient is stunned and sits and listens.

Do you assist in the admission process at the treatment center?

The interventionist should help accomplish a smooth transition from the intervention close into the admission process. Most interventionists will walk patients and family members through the admission process.

What can a family member do at the home site to ensure an intervention will go smoothly?

Most interventionists instruct you in detail what to do. Examples are: Take the phone off the hook; be certain infants who might start to cry are in another room with someone present to see to their needs; put dogs, cats, and other domestic pets outside.

Will you abort a scheduled intervention?

If the person being intervened with is too much under the influence of drugs to respond, an interventionist should be willing to abort and reschedule the intervention. Also, the person initiating the intervention should have the option to abort it at any stage of the process.

What do participants typically feel before, during, and after an intervention?

After the preparation meeting, you should feel ready and eager to intervene. At the actual start of the intervention, there is usually some anxiety, which passes quickly. At the end of the intervention, you will feel relief and pride.

What's the ideal number of participants in an intervention?

There is no set rule. It's quality, not quantity, that counts.

Are participants who have addictive diseases themselves allowed to participate?

If an addicted participant might warn the person being intervened with about the intervention, most interventionists feel he or she should not participate. The final criterion is the degree of trust the family feels toward a given participant.

Can young children participate in an intervention?

Yes. But most interventionists will request an opportunity to assess whether their participation is appropriate. Letters written by children and read by the interventionist are often an effective substitute for their actual participation.

If a key participant can't attend the preparation meeting, can that person participate in the intervention?

Yes—if an interventionist is willing to prepare the participant by phone and agrees to his or her participation.

Can two family members be intervened with on the same day?

Some interventionists have a method to orchestrate this. Usually an interventionist will intervene with one in the morning and the other in the afternoon.

Do you have to have a bottom-line consequence such as job termination, separation, or divorce to ensure the success of an intervention?

Many interventionists feel this is necessary only in extremely difficult cases. Most interventions never reach the "or else" stage. The primary goal in intervention is to present the addicted person with a solution to the problem, and to give the families and friends the peace that comes with having acted and knowing they have done their best.

Appendix B:
The Treatment Center

I am often asked why addicted people should enter treatment centers, why they can't recover from addiction without going to a facility where they must remain as an inpatient for twenty-eight to thirty-five days.

I never look upon a treatment center as a place of confinement where one *must* stay. I look upon it as a haven, a place for healing where people who have difficulty overcoming denial of their addiction or passivity about confronting it can be guided in taking essential steps toward restoration of their physical, spiritual, and mental well-being.

Within the cocoonlike, sheltered environment of a treatment center, the addicted are taught to face themselves, their disease, and their frustrations with life as they are weaned from the mood-altering chemicals and/or aberrant behavior they have used to soften or mask pain.

The ideal treatment facility is an attractive, well-maintained structure that contains adequate quarters for its medical, counseling, and support staff and provides comfortable living accommodations that impart maximum privacy from the outside world, but exposure to the healing inner world of the center.

The ideal treatment center staff is made up of skilled helping professionals from different disciplines who interact purposefully to motivate patients toward recovery.

It always interests me when at the end of a stay in a good treatment center patients say, "It didn't even matter what drug I was addicted to. My program negated my self-destructive habits, restored my zest and energy to pursue positive goals in life."

What follows is a generalized description of the components of a good comprehensive treatment center program and a list of things families, friends, or colleagues might want to think about or discuss with intake counselors either on the phone or during a personal tour of a facility.

THE COURSE OF TREATMENT

PRE-ADMISSION

Bearing in mind that some forms require patient approval and signature, once arrangements for an intervention are under way, family members and/or employers should receive the full support and cooperation of the intake/admission staff of a treatment center in accomplishing everything possible to ease the admission process for the patient. This includes receiving treatment center staff assistance in these areas:

- Verifying insurance coverage

- Determining the responsible person's payment obligation

- Completing release of medical information forms that will enable the medical staff at the treatment center to have access to the patient's previous medical records from outside physicians

- Completing a medical history which specifies what medicines the incoming patient regularly takes for conditions such as high blood pressure, diabetes, or epilepsy. (When possible, family members should take prescription medicines with them at the time of admission. The medicines will then be administered at the appropriate times by nurses and physicians.)

- With the patient's permission, completing "release of confidentiality" forms which list the names of people who will be allowed to receive information about the patient once the patient is admitted

- Filling out as fully as possible any required release forms the patient must sign at the time of admission so that all that is required from the patient at that time is his or her signature and an oral explanation of the release form's contents

INTAKE AND ADMISSION

Because admission is usually the patient's first exposure to the treatment center, this interval can be critical in shaping patient attitudes—especially when patients, because of their emotional and/or physical state, may be resistant to answering questions. Even with thorough pre-admission arrangements, there are often unexpected questions that arise or insurance documents to be reconfirmed.

It is therefore essential, especially in difficult cases, that family members, employers, and associates satisfy themselves ahead of time that all those on the treatment center staff—administrators and counselors, doctors and nurses, insurance processors and billing personnel—will do their utmost to instill confidence.

Most treatment centers do have empathic staff members who make the admission process as painless as possible. Family members should sense that empathy when touring a facility, or, if they are unable to visit personally, have it affirmed by someone familiar with the center.

Whenever it's feasible during intake/admission, I request that patients be taken directly to their assigned rooms in the primary care/detoxification unit while I remain at the admitting desk with family members to help with the necessary paperwork and make certain family members are treated respectfully.

PRIMARY CARE/DETOXIFICATION

Detoxification procedures vary from center to center. However, as a general rule, the entering patient is taken directly to his or her room in the detoxification unit where nurses and doctors with extensive experience in chemical dependency make certain the patient's withdrawal from alcohol or other chemicals is safe and painless. A nurse will take vital signs and a drinking/drug and physical history. A staff physician will do a complete physical examination, and standing orders from that physician will immediately be put into effect. If family members aren't acquainted with a staff physician, the head nurse is an excellent person to ask to recommend one.

With some patients, Librium is used to ease withdrawal;

with others, Valium. With still others, there is no need for detoxification medication of any kind. If patients are using prescription drugs, detoxification may take longer than it would otherwise. Once a patient's vital signs become stable, all withdrawal-easing medication is stopped.

The medical aspects of addiction are focused on during primary care/detoxification, so although the environment is comfortable, it is, of necessity, medical. Usually no telephone calls in or out of the facility are permitted during detoxification. Patients requiring intensive care or special medical treatment will be monitored around the clock, or transferred to the ICU (intensive care unit) of an adjunct hospital.

Detoxification nurses and counselors concentrate on diminishing patient anxiety during the first twenty-four to seventy-two hours. To help accomplish this, patients are taken on a tour of the facility and given books and pamphlets to read describing the treatment program.

The patient's primary counselor introduces himself or herself to the patient on the first or second day and conducts psychological/sociological tests to establish treatment priorities.

A "buddy" relationship with another recovering patient who has successfully gone through the detoxification process and is able to instill confidence and hope will be encouraged.

Because of the psychological as well as physical stress patients may undergo during detoxification, specially skilled nurses or counselors are often assigned to spend private one-on-one time talking to new patients. A comforting conversation often eases fear and anxiety more than medication.

Some patients will experience a surprising surge of physical well-being after withdrawal that may cause them to say, "Gosh, I feel so good, I'm ready to leave." Should this happen, family members and/or employers should be prepared to reinforce the treatment center staff's insistence that long-term work is necessary to recovery.

Should patients become agitated and attempt to leave the facility AMA (against medical advice), the entire staff will unite to motivate that patient to remain in treatment, and family members and/or employers should be prepared to support that effort. Staff members in a treatment center regard leaving AMA as the equivalent of a Code Blue in a general hospital. They know if the patient leaves AMA, he or she will have another chemical-dependency crisis within a short time.

Addictive people are skillful manipulators and will sometimes try to pit one staff member against another, and to draw family members, friends, and employers into the fray. The multidisciplinary approach that characterizes a good treatment center defeats such tactics while nurturing patient awareness and acceptance of the long-term work recovery entails. Here again, cooperation of family, friends, and employers is essential.

Time spent in primary care or detox is usually two to four days, depending on the severity and physical effects of the addiction.

REHABILITATION

The cocoonlike environment of rehabilitation is the heart of the inpatient program. This is where the satellite issues of life—jobs, financial obligations, relationships, holidays the rest of the world may be celebrating or catastrophes it may be enduring—are not allowed to intrude.

Patients are offered time, space, and empathy to attain attitudes of admission and compliance that will ensure their recovery. They must become willing to admit they have the disease of addiction and that it has made their lives unmanageable, and then comply with activities that will alter the life patterns that have perpetuated the disease.

Family, friends, and employers must understand treatment center personnel are doing their utmost to keep patients focused on the work of recovery. Telephones and television sets are not permitted in patients' rooms. Reading newspapers and magazines and watching TV are limited to restricted periods in recreation rooms. Patients are expected to follow a daily routine designed to foster self-discipline and help them accept responsibility for their own mental and physical well-being. This routine begins with an activity as simple as having the patient get up in the morning and eat a nutritious breakfast—something most addicted people have long since ceased doing. It gradually broadens to include having patients:

- do their own laundry.

- keep their rooms neat and clean.

- take part in recreational therapy (aerobics, walking, jogging, weight training, physical exercise) to rejuvenate their bodies.

- participate in one-on-one counseling sessions with the primary counselor.

- focus on overcoming fear and frustration through self-exploration.

- complete written assignments each night to be discussed with the primary counselor the next morning or during a special session set aside for this purpose.

- take part in group therapy sessions led by a recovering degreed therapist, or a family member of a recovering person who is astute at group dynamics. (So much fear and anxiety is resolved during these group sessions and they are considered so crucial to the recovery process that even physicians may not summon patients out of such meetings.)

- attend educational classes to learn about the obsessive-compulsive and biochemical aspects of addiction, as well as the tendency to become cross-addicted to such things as eating, sugar, gambling, or destructive relationships.

- enrich their spirituality and serenity through meditation, discussion with religious counselors at the center, or being accompanied to services outside the center.

- become aware of those spiritual concepts that lead into participation in "anonymous" groups and acceptance of the Twelve Steps (see Appendix C).

- attend special men's and women's therapy sessions in which sexual fears and anxieties are explored in segregated groups.

- participate in counseling sessions with family members. (These patient/family sessions focus on both education about addiction and exploration of family patterns that may have perpetuated the disease.)

- interact with an increasing number of recovering patients and other patients' family members to achieve emotional bonding with as many people involved in the recovery process as possible.

- become involved with an ongoing self-help community support group, which may be allied to but exist separately from the treatment center. (All comprehensive treatment centers interweave the steps of the anonymous groups— Alcoholics Anonymous, Cocaine Anonymous, Narcotics Anonymous, etc.—into their therapeutic activities. Many centers take patients on special trips to visit anonymous groups so patients may experience firsthand what happens at such meetings.)

Mastering this routine provides a smooth transition into the next stage of recovery, aftercare.

AFTERCARE

Aftercare commences when the patient leaves the treatment center and begins resuming his or her daily life activities.

Many treatment facilities offer aftercare sessions one or two nights a week for as long as a year after inpatient treatment ends. These sessions not only reinforce the regime and activities begun during rehabilitation, but also strengthen connection to an anonymous self-help group separate from the treatment center. Self-help groups are uniquely effective in helping people in recovery maintain abstinence. Unlike other therapeutic doctrines which assert, "You come to us, and we'll change your thinking and therefore your actions will change," self-help philosophy asserts, "You come to us, and we'll change your actions and therefore your thinking will change." Connection to anonymous self-help groups is essential to many people to ensure their continued progress toward recovery.

THINGS FOR FAMILY MEMBERS TO OBSERVE AND/OR INQUIRE ABOUT

THE TREATMENT FACILITY

A personal tour of a facility will reveal whether it comfortably houses its medical, counseling, and service staff and provides cheerful and attractive living accommodations for patients. A telephone conversation with an intake counselor and perusal of a treatment center's brochures can provide similar information.

Specific considerations sometimes influence people to choose a particular facility. Being within easy driving distance for visitation and participation in family sessions may be one. Association with a hospital that can treat a patient whose physical health has been severely impaired may be another.

Psychiatrists are not on staff at all treatment centers. Any family desiring in-depth psychiatric consultation for their loved one should find out beforehand whether a psychiatrist is on staff or available on an on-call basis.

It's wise to ask what clothing patients should bring and what the visiting hours are. Visiting may be carefully monitored, especially at the beginning, to avoid emotional confrontations with family members or even the possibility of drugs being smuggled in.

It's my personal belief that a treatment center should be able to admit a patient involved in chemical dependency crisis any time of the day or night, on weekdays or on Saturdays or Sundays, just as a comprehensive medical/surgical hospital does. However, some treatment centers close their admissions offices from 3:00 P.M. on Friday until 9:00 A.M. on Monday. Therefore, it's always wise to inquire what admitting hours are and whether exceptions are made for emergencies.

Beyond these specific considerations, factors such as the ambience, the grounds, and the view are meaningful only insofar as they may instill or increase the confidence and positive feelings of patients and/or their families.

Occasionally, people will go "facility shopping" with a long list of things they feel might benefit their loved one. I've been asked whether swimming pools, Jacuzzis, horseback riding, and tennis courts are available. There are luxurious facilities that have some or all of these things. However, it's important to understand that all the stages of treatment I have outlined can take place in facilities large or small, urban or rural, luxuriously or modestly appointed, expensive or moderately priced, ranging in cost from $4,000 to $50,000.

QUESTIONS TO ASK THE STAFF IN GENERAL

A rule of thumb: If you do not receive immediate positive feedback from any staff member you encounter when visiting a facility, that person is not doing his or her job. It's always unfortunate when a visiting family member is made uneasy by a staff member who behaves unprofessionally, uses too many technical words, is curt in responding to questions, or falls short in some other way. However, a single individual's shortcomings should not make you conclude that the facility isn't a good one. Speak to an administrator about any doubts or uneasiness you may be experiencing.

If you ask any staff member what his or her philosophy of treatment is, that person's reply should encompass the physical, psychological, and spiritual well-being of patients. Be warned—some staff members are so warmly enthusiastic and well informed that they may go on at considerable length.

In addition to inquiring about treatment philosophy, you may wish to ask:

- How long, on the average, have staff members remained at the facility? (I'm always impressed when staff members stay five years or longer, and concerned when turnover is high.)

- What is the percentage of patients who have completed treatment? (A high percentage is an indication of an excellent staff.)

- How many staff members are themselves recovering from addiction; how many of the staff are family members who were former enablers; how many of the staff are adult children of alcoholics?

- What is the counselor/patient ratio? (One counselor to six or eight patients is a good ratio. One counselor to ten patients is the maximum acceptable. Generally, the counselor/patient ratio is smaller in inpatient programs than it is at outpatient programs.)

- How are calls from employers or business associates handled by staff? (It has been my experience that employers in general are highly supportive of employees who enter treatment and their calls are intelligently handled by the treatment center staff.)

QUESTIONS TO ASK ABOUT DETOXIFICATION

- How long have the nurses and doctors in the detoxification unit been working in the field of chemical dependency?

- Do they wean patients off detoxification medication as quickly as possible?

- Does the detoxification staff—while treating medical aspects of addiction—encourage patients to be aware of longer-term aspects of recovery, the biochemical/compulsive-obsessive aspects of the disease, and the twelve-step recovery program advocated by the anonymous self-help groups?

- Will the results of the patient's physical examination at the center be made available to the family? (Often the center's examining physician doesn't provide that information unless it is specifically requested.)

QUESTIONS TO ASK ABOUT REHABILITATION

- What techniques does the primary counselor use to achieve bonding with the patient?

- What psychological or sociological tests are used to create a personalized treatment plan?

- Are mood-altering drugs administered during rehab? (They shouldn't be.)

- How frequently does the patient have one-on-one sessions with the primary counselor?

- What is the daily schedule during rehabilitation?

- Is there a nutritionist on the staff? Is there vitamin therapy? Is the dietary plan available for review?

- What physical and recreational activities are available? If an individual isn't physically able to participate in the physical-exercise regime, are there alternative activities offered?

- What types of spiritual guidance are offered? Are clergymen of different faiths available? Are lectures given on spiritual growth?

- Are four-hour passes given? How successfully have they been used? (This is a controversial issue at this time.)

- How many days is the average patient in rehabilitation before family counseling begins, and how often are family sessions held? Who is the family therapist? What responsibilities will family members be expected to assume for themselves during counseling?

QUESTIONS TO ASK ABOUT AFTERCARE

- Does an aftercare program exist? (Unfortunately, some treatment centers don't provide adequate people to staff an aftercare program.)

- How often are meetings held?

- What are the meetings focused on?

- Are both patients and family members included? Do they meet separately, together, or both?

- What is the rate of attendance at aftercare programs by patients who have left the treatment center? (If the treatment center has done its job and the aftercare program is a good one, attendance will be high.)

- During aftercare, is connection to one of the anonymous self-help groups separate from the treatment center strengthened and encouraged?

- If an out-of-state treatment center is selected, does that center have a reciprocal agreement with a local facility that has an aftercare program?

- Beyond aftercare, does the treatment center have an alumni group? (A comprehensive treatment center will have a strong and active alumni group.)

QUESTIONS INTERVENTIONISTS ARE FREQUENTLY ASKED ABOUT TREATMENT CENTERS

What is the rationale underlying programs that require only a short-term inpatient stay?

Short-term programs may be appropriate for people who are already sincerely motivated to begin recovery and people who have relapsed and require an intensive short-term course of recovery treatment. Also, they are certainly better than nothing for people who can't afford a long-term program or whose insurance coverage will pay only for a short-term program. And when followed by an intensive aftercare program fostering connection to one of the anonymous self-help groups, a short-term program can be very effective.

Why aren't outpatient programs as effective as inpatient programs?

Emotional bonding among patients and other people involved in the treatment process is widely acknowledged to be a primary activator of recovery. There is a much greater opportunity for such bonding to occur among people who live together twenty-four hours a day for twenty-eight to thirty-five days than there is among people who see each other two to three hours in the evening, following days filled with normal work and family activities.

A simple mathematical calculation makes it clear that to obtain 480 hours of treatment as an outpatient, it would take twenty-four weeks at five nights a week, four hours a night, whereas 480 hours of treatment as an inpatient can be obtained in thirty days, sixteen hours a day.

I do want to make it clear that some outpatient programs are excellent. Those which are require a thorough examination by the program's physician, attendance at daily or nightly sessions, completion of homework assignments, family participation, abstention from alcohol and/or drugs, and random drug screening to confirm patients are remaining off mood-altering substances.

Since treatment centers strongly stress leading patients into anonymous self-help groups, why shouldn't patients simply start out in such self-help groups?

Few people I have intervened with were capable of making the strong commitment to the activities required by the Twelve Steps of the anonymous groups without first having been exposed to the psychological and educational preparation which took place in the treatment center.

However, patients who are sincerely and deeply motivated to recovery can and do find what they need by joining a self-help group on their own.

The Twelve Steps required by the anonymous groups are designed to change the person's life-style and behavior through changing his or her actions. Many addicted people don't attend self-help group meetings long enough to acquire the habit of performing the actions that result in behavioral change. However, after completing an inpatient program in a treatment center—which usually entails working through the first three steps of self-help group philosophy, and being introduced to the other nine—the recovering patient will have acquired habits of action that will enable him or her to work through the remaining self-help steps to recovery. (See Appendix C for a complete listing of the Twelve Steps.)

> *Should someone who has completed an inpatient treatment program and then has a relapse enter an inpatient treatment center again?*

I believe treatment centers should accommodate patients who have previously gone through treatment with modified and streamlined programs that focus on restabilizing the recovery process and restrengthening the connection to a self-help group and therapist.

More and more facilities are devoting special attention to relapse, and special methods of treating it are developing rapidly.

> *How is the family brought into counseling?*

A family counseling coordinator conducts an orientation for the patient's family and informs the family when family counseling will begin.

> *Will Medicare cover costs of inpatient treatment?*

Medicare rules and regulations change frequently. Contact a treatment center in your area to find out what the current Medicare criteria are.

> *Will CHAMPUS (government employee insurance) cover the cost of inpatient treatment?*

CHAMPUS will cover treatment costs for alcoholism and other chemical dependencies. An intake counselor can answer questions covering CHAMPUS protocol and the paperwork required, and treatment facility requirements.

Will treatment facilities accept cash payments?

Intake counselors at any facility will outline their cash payment schedules for prospective clients.

Are there any low-cost or free treatment programs?

Low-cost or free state-run programs are available to addicted people who are able and willing to abide by their rules and regulations. However, there is frequently a long list of people waiting to be admitted, and those who are must be motivated toward recovery before they enter the program.

Social model and therapeutic communities are also viable places for low-cost treatment. They stress psychological, educational, and spiritual aspects of recovery. They detox nonmedically (although if someone has difficulty, they will take that person to a hospital emergency room). They do excellent work in getting people to abstain from mood-altering drugs and affiliate with aftercare programs or self-help groups to sustain recovery.

Although it isn't widely known, there are low-cost recovery houses and halfway houses available for men and women who require a stabilization period before reentering family life and reassuming family responsibilities.

There are also longer-term living facilities available for people recovering from addiction. These facilities have sliding scales of payment based on ability to pay.

What will insurance companies pay toward the cost of treatment?

It varies widely. Many insurance plans will pay 50, 80, or 100 percent of inpatient and/or outpatient treatment costs. Some insurance companies reject certain treatment facilities but will pay for treatment at others. Thorough investigation is often necessary to ascertain exactly what a given insurance company will cover.

Are there any independent agencies that monitor treatment centers and provide unbiased reports about how well they provide the services they promise?

A major monitoring agency is the Joint Commission Accreditation of Hospitals (which monitors all hospitals). Many insurance companies demand this accreditation.

However, I feel it is important to remember that the product of a treatment center is treatment. If a treatment center is doing its job, that will be affirmed through referrals from patients and its verifiable reputation.

Appendix C:
The Twelve Steps

Here are the steps that are suggested as a program of recovery.

1. We admitted we were powerless over alcohol—that our lives had become unmanageable.

2. Came to believe that a Power greater than ourselves could restore us to sanity.

3. Made a decision to turn our will and our lives over to the care of God *as we understood Him.*

4. Made a searching and fearless moral inventory of ourselves.

5. Admitted to God, to ourselves, and to another human being the exact nature of our wrongs.

6. Were entirely ready to have God remove all these defects of character.

7. Humbly asked Him to remove our shortcomings.

8. Made a list of all persons we had harmed, and became willing to make amends to them all.

9. Made direct amends to such people wherever possible, except when to do so would injure them or others.

10. Continued to take personal inventory and when we were wrong promptly admitted it.

11. Sought through prayer and meditation to improve our conscious contact with God *as we understood Him,* praying

The Twelve Steps are reprinted with permission of Alcoholics Anonymous World Services, Inc.

only for knowledge of His will for us and the power to carry that out.

12. Having had a spiritual awakening as the result of these steps, we tried to carry this message to alcoholics, and to practice these principles in all our affairs.

Appendix D:
Addresses of Treatment Centers

Following is a list of treatment centers and medical corporations that provide comprehensive care, have interventionists on staff, or will make referrals to outside interventionists.

Please be aware that in addition to those on this list there are many additional treatment centers with qualified interventionists on staff.

MEDICAL CORPORATIONS WITH TREATMENT CENTERS NATIONWIDE

Comprehensive Care
    Corporation
2101 E. Fourth Street,
Suite 185
Santa Ana, CA 92705
(Network of 240 centers)
800-321-8669

Charter Medical
    Corporation
Addictive Disease Division
11050 Crab Apple Road,
Suite D-120
Roswell, GA 30075
(50 hospitals nationwide)
800-845-1567

Parkside Medical Services
Park Ridge, IL
(Network of 60 centers)
312-698-4700

Koala Centers
Nashville, TN
(Network of 40 centers in
    10 states)
615-665-1144

New Beginnings
1010 Wisconsin Avenue,
    N.W.
Washington, DC 20007
(42 centers nationwide)
202-298-3230
714-581-1445

TREATMENT CENTERS IN INDIVIDUAL STATES

ALASKA

North Point–Milam
    Recovery Center, Inc.
4426 Wright Street
Anchorage, AK 99507
907-562-4011

Juneau, AK
907-780-4948

Fairbanks, AK
907-479-4476

ARIZONA

Cottonwood
4110 Sweetwater Drive
Tucson, AZ 85745
602-743-0411

CALIFORNIA

Betty Ford Center
at Eisenhower
Rancho Mirage, CA
800-392-7540—California
800-854-9211—out of
state

Community Hospital
Recovery Center
576 Hartnell Street
Monterey, CA 93940
408-373-0924
800-528-8080

Forrest Farm
145 Tamal Road
P.O. Box 279
Forrest Knolls, CA 94933
415-488-9287

Long Beach Memorial
Coastview
Adult and Adolescent
Chemical Dependency
Unit
Memorial Medical Center
of Long Beach
455 Columbia Street
Long Beach, CA 90801
213-426-6619

Medical Center of Garden
Grove
Eating Disorders Center
12601 Garden Grove
Boulevard
Garden Grove, CA 92643
714-537-5160

Mt. Diablo Hospital
Medical Center
2540 East Street
Concord, CA 94520-1960
415-674-2200

Monte Villa Hospital
1729 Hale Avenue
Morgan Hill, CA 95037
408-779-4151

GEORGIA

Willingway
311 Jones Mill Road
Stateboro, GA 30458
800-235-0790
912-764-6236

MAINE

Mediplex Group, Inc.
15 Walnut Street
Wellesley, ME 02181
(Also in New York, New
Hampshire, Virginia,
Kansas)
617-446-6900

MARYLAND

Ashley
Havre de Grace, MD
301-273-6600

MINNESOTA

Hazelden
Center City, MN
612-257-4010, Ext. 3307
800-262-5010

St. Mary's Chemical
  Dependency Service
2512 South 7th Street
Minneapolis, MN 55454
612-337-4400

MISSOURI

Hyland Center
10020 Kennerly Road
St. Louis, MO 63128
314-525-7200

NEW JERSEY

Fair Oaks Hospital
19 Prospect Street
Summit, NJ 07901
201-522-7000

NEW MEXICO

Cottonwood
P.O. Box 1270
Los Lunas, NM 87031
505-865-3345

NEW YORK

Benjamin Rush Center
672 S. Salina Street
Syracuse, NY 13202
312-476-2161

Smithers Alcoholism
  and Treatment Center
428 West 59th Street
New York, NY 10019
212-554-6491
212-554-6577

South Oaks Hospital
400 Sunrise Highway
Amityville, NY 11701

OREGON

Serenity Lane
616 East 16th
Eugene, OR 97401
503-687-1110

PENNSYLVANIA

Chit Chat Treatment
  Centers
Werners Ville, PA
215-678-2332

Marworth
Adolescent and Adult
  Chemical Dependency
  Treatment Center
Shawnee on Delaware, PA
717-424-8065 (adolescent)
717-563-1112 (adult)

RHODE ISLAND

Edgehill Newport
Newport, RI
(Also in New York, New
  Jersey)
800-252-6466
401-849-5700

WASHINGTON

Meridian
P.O. Box 863
Lynden, WA 98264
(Servicing Canadian
  referrals)
206-354-4050

Milam Recovery Centers,
  Inc.
14500 Juanita Drive N.E.
Bothell, WA 98011
206-823-3116

WISCONSIN

DePaul Rehabilitation
  Hospital
4143 South 13th Street
Milwaukee,WI 53221
414-281-4400